that *i* might not sin

Equipping Today's Children for Tomorrow's Challenges

A values-based scripture memory book for children,
with weekly devotions for the whole family.

robin newman

TATE PUBLISHING, LLC

Published in the United States of America
by Tate Publishing, LLC
127 East Trade Center Terrace
Mustang, OK 73064
(888) 361–9473

ISBN: 1–9332907–2-2

**Thy Word have I hidden in my heart,
that I might not sin against God.**

Psalm 119:11

Dedication

This book is lovingly dedicated to my parents, Ken and Addie Robinson. Without their support and their incredible encouragement over the years as I pursued my dreams of writing, this book would never be a reality.

Thank you Mom and Dad for the time you so selflessly gave to help with the kids, meals, and laundry when I had more to do than I could ever conceive of accomplishing. Through your sacrificial gifts and through your prayers on my behalf, the Lord has brought to fruition this book. . . . in His time.

Dear Haley and Anna
I hope this book will be of
value to you as you grow in
your knowledge of His ways.

I love you!
Granddaddy

Acknowledgements

I want to lovingly acknowledge those that have had an impact whether directly or indirectly with the outcome and process of this book:

To my husband: Thank you for waiting up long hours of the night with me as I wrote, for giving me the time I needed, doing extra "daddy duties," and for being the spiritual leader of our home. Oh yeah, I guess your savvy computer skills helped a little too. How many times did I yell a desperate "HELP!" or call you in for "just a quick question"? Without a doubt, this work would not be in print today without your knowledge of everything related to the computer. Your love sustains me.

To my children: Joshua, Jordan and Brooklyn: Here it is, kids. "The book" I was working on so many Saturdays and evenings when all you wanted to do was play with mom. You were patient beyond your years as I turned down too many offers of "Yatzee," "Skip- Bo" and trips to the park and library to spend time writing. Thank you for being so incredibly kind about my many "not right nows." How 'bout a game of "Sorry"?

To my parents: Without the constant example you have been through the years, the very essence of this book would not exist. It was through your modeling Christ in the home that I learned the importance of devotions, prayer, and scripture memory while growing up.

To my dear friend and college roommate, Beth Henry: Thank you for your ever constant belief in me and in this entire process. Your faithfulness and prayers lifted me numerous times.

To Tara and Melanie: Again, always there, always asking, always encouraging. Thank you.

To Christie, Cathy, Vicki, and Diane: The meals were wonderful, the prayers out of this world. I couldn't have done it without you that week.

"the shema": to shout
Parent's Creed

Hear, O Israel: The LORD our God, the LORD is one. Love the LORD your God with all your heart and with all your soul and with all your strength. These commandments that I give you today are to be upon your hearts. Impress them on your children. Talk about them when you sit at home and when you walk along the road, when you lie down and when you get up.

(Deuteronomy 6:4-7)

Table of Contents

Foreword for Parents: The Importance of Scripture Memory

Have you ever had the feeling of being isolated from the world around you because you lacked some aspect of modern technology? It seems we have become so accustomed to having technology at our fingertips that we find it hard to survive when the media isn't so accessible to us, if even for a day. Media instantly affords us the luxury of being in touch with our community and our world where news can change on an hourly basis.

Imagine if you will then, life without God's Word, the Bible. If scripture was somehow lost, buried, or hidden away from our sight, truths that are revealed only in scripture could not be easily taught to a young, eager audience. How could we find strength for the trials that so often beset us? And how would our children learn to cope with pressure from the world? Where would their basis for morality originate without the insight of scripture? As Christians, the scriptures are our foundation to the reason behind what we do, say, and think. Without the guidance of God's Word, morality does not exist. I believe that an existence without His Word would be far worse than a day without the high tech industry.

As parents, the Bible is our most valuable resource when it comes to raising our children with values, character, and discipline. It is our duty, if not our privilege, to share the knowledge of scripture with this younger generation living in our very shadows. We must discover how to incorporate scripture into our daily conversations with them. We need to show them the relevance of scripture in their lives. Providing even small morsels of truth each day can reinforce biblical values which can be tucked away and carried with them wherever they go.

By helping our children memorize scripture, we will be equipping them with a life-long gift of wisdom and strength as they leave our protective side and face the world on their own. We will be giving them a wealth of resources on which to draw when they need it most. Whether 3 or 13, children are never too young or too old to hide God's rich truths in their hearts.

Memorization is an asset which allows for quick referencing. It also provides a well-spring of encouragement and insight that can be at our fingertips when other resources cannot. We teach our children early on about such conveniences as computers, cell phones, IPods, and television. Modern technology is at the heart of the secular world today . . . but at the heart of every Christian home, God's Word should be found. While teaching our children about technology, let us not neglect to also teach them about our greatest media masterpiece yet: God's Word.

How To Use This Book

*To begin scripture memory with your child, first and foremost begin with prayer, asking God to reveal the importance of His Word to you and your family.

*Become familiar with the book, its structure and its contents before trying to incorporate it into your child's life.

*Decide how you would like to use the book and what you hope to accomplish through using it. The book is organized according to months of the year (often coinciding with special holidays and events) and grouped in thematic chapters. Perhaps you would prefer to follow a thematic approach, disregarding the system of months outlined. The topics are not contingent upon each other; hence, moving around depending on your family's needs and interest is a viable option. Or perhaps following it from cover to cover suits you best. However, how you choose to use it is up to you.

*After deciding which method works best for you, it's time to begin an exciting adventure of discovering God's truth and helping make it relevant for your child. After choosing where you wish to begin, you will find the overall topic that you have chosen with an attached story to be read to your child. This simply introduces him to what the entire month will be focusing on. A few general questions will follow, allowing your child to move into a deeper thinking strategy about the chosen theme. For young pre-schoolers, you may opt out of the question at this level. Whatever they can grasp now will be sufficient.

*On the following page you will find the specific topic of the week. Each weekly topic will correspond with the unit theme. The chosen verse, story, and activity should all center on this topic. It will begin with the verse to be memorized. Only one verse per week will be given unless otherwise stated. However, if a greater challenge is needed, you can use the reference verses provided at the end of each week to gather further verses for memorization.

*Because of varying preferences, you will find that both the NIV and the KJV have been printed for each verse that is to be memorized. If KJV is preferred, then omit the NIV text and focus only on the verse marked KJV. Oftentimes the verses are exactly the same. Other times you may find such a vast difference that you wish to "cross over" and memorize from a version other than what you have been using.

*As you begin the week's topic, read the verse to your child or have him read it aloud to you. Locating it and then reading it from the Bible is a good way to demonstrate to children that the verse being memorized originated from God's Word rather than just another book from the bookshelf. Ask for your child's thoughts on the verse. Often, they may not have any related thoughts to share. Other times, their interpretation of the verse may not be the intended meaning. At this point, that is okay. We are just exploring ideas and brainstorming at this time. Allow for any thoughts they may have including any "wrong" ideas. Children need to feel safe in their attempt to understand scripture. Avoid the temptation to correct too soon, mistakenly causing them to feel "bad" for misunderstanding God's Word. As adults, we too are still learning and trying to understand the depth of His Word.

*After having read the verse, follow with the story. This should help reinforce the relevance of the verse and how to apply scripture to life today.

*Ask the questions following the story, again allowing room for individual responses, but correcting their misunderstandings if needed.

*Read the memory verse again, this time providing an explanation if needed. Replacing general pronouns with your child's own name or even relating it to personal experiences that have recently occurred will help bring the verse to life, allowing for greater understanding.

Practice quoting the scripture verse in small segments, then as a whole several times. For younger children, an asterisk follows the portion of scripture which may be more appropriate for them to memorize. Work with what your child is capable of handling regardless of his or her age. Scripture memory is not intended to add extra stress to a child's life. If the longer verse is too much, then shorten it to make it compatible with your needs. You are certainly not bound by these guidelines.

*After reciting the verse, pray the accompanied prayer with your child, or if you prefer, pray your own prayer with your child.

*You will notice a family activity has been included at the end of each week's focus. This is provided for those who want extra reinforcement throughout the week. You might even want to sing a song that corresponds to the topic or see if you and your family can make one up together. Have fun with the activities and units. Use it as a time to draw closer to the Lord as well as your own family.

*For the remainder of the nights during the week, I would invite you to come together as a family whenever possible, reviewing the verse, talking about its meaning in relation to life today, and researching the other references provided on the same subject. The references are furnished as a cross-reference devotional tool to reinforce the value of the week. Look up the verses and discuss them together. For younger children, this may be too much. If older children are participating, have each family member use his or her own Bible to locate and read the verses. Obviously, younger children cannot do this on their own. Perhaps an older child can help the younger ones find the verse. Finding verses as a family is a wonderful learning/teaching opportunity regardless of the ages involved. It helps everyone become familiar with the Bible, and it also shows them that Mom and Dad value God's Word. Children imitate *what* we do much more than what we *tell* them to do. After reading and discussing the verses, always end in prayer, remembering especially to pray for your children by name.

*In Deuteronomy 6 we are admonished to teach the scriptures to our children. We are told to talk about them at home, on the road, at bedtime and when we awake. I encourage you to follow the same guidelines in memorizing the verses outlined in this book. Repetition is a child's best friend. Since children do not quickly grow tired of repetition, seize every opportunity to review the verses: in the car, at the dinner table, while shopping, bathing, or even while praying. The more they hear something, the more likely it is to remain with them.

*Scripture memory takes time. It cannot be haphazardly approached for success to occur. You must commit to it like anything else, and then follow through with your commitment. Finding the time is not easy. Some nights will seem impossible to work it in to your schedule. Don't allow yourself to fret over the availability of time. But, if you make it a priority and purposely set aside the time, it is more likely to occur on a regular basis and eventually become a habit. As success is achieved, you and your child will be more motivated to participate.

*Children will find it easier to memorize scripture if they see the importance of it or find value in it. If they understand what is being memorized and how it relates to them, it too will have more meaning in their life and be retained quicker. Finally, the more they hear the verse, the better able they will be to commit it to memory.

*I recommend choosing one night a week to work on the verse, read the story and discuss the associated value. Use the other evenings to review, enhance and discuss verses associated with the weekly theme.

* At the end of the week, use the "tear out" chart found in the back of the book as a visual aid to keep record of verses learned and to motivate further learning. Stickers, stars, or a

check mark placed in each box as the verse is committed to memory works well as a positive reinforcement tool.

    * Keep in mind the goal of scripture memory, which is stated so eloquently in Psalm 119:11:

    "Thy word have I hid in my heart, that I might not sin against thee."

    * It is more important to take the time to learn one verse than to stick to a rigid schedule, only to discover later that few verses have been retained and understood. God's Word holds a wealth of wisdom for those who dare seek the deeper treasures waiting to be discovered. It is my prayer that this book would not so much be seen as a goal to be conquered, but as part of a life-long journey with truths waiting to be revealed.

Leading Your Child To Christ

"Thank you God for the pretty flowers, and juice, and all the little bugs, and my bed, and for red crayons. Amen."

Ahh, the simplicity of a child's prayer—prayers straight from the heart. They cover the gamut of life as their words tickle our ears with the purest of innocence. As parents we laugh in awe at such honest prayers. But it seems that before we even have a chance to decipher their meaning, those same children are asking probing questions about the essence of our faith. As parents, we too often find ourselves wondering how we will know when our child is ready to accept Christ as Savior, and what the proper age is. Sadly, we discover that we lack the confidence, if not the knowledge, to lead our own child to a saving faith in Christ.

Because salvation is the single most important decision our children will ever make, it is imperative that we have a basic understanding of how to lead them to Christ as well as knowing when they are ready to commit their hearts to Jesus.

Jesus plainly tells us that we all must have the faith of a child or "child-like faith" in order to receive eternal life. He admonished His disciples to bring the little children to Him and never hinder one from coming to His side. In fact, they were rebuked for trying to keep the children away. Jesus loves children and knows the heart of a child far better than we. He will guide us at the right time, but until then, we don't have to sit idly by hoping that someday our child will want to accept Jesus as Savior. Several steps will assist us in being prepared for that moment.

*Recognize that every child needs the love of God and that no child is ever too old or too "bad" to come to the throne of God.

*Pray daily for the salvation of each of your children, even as infants.

*Pray that you will be guided in wisdom and speech as you explain salvation to your child at a level appropriate for him or her.

*Pray that as the Holy Spirit convicts their hearts, they will surrender to him.

*Daily model the importance of Jesus in your own life.

*Freely talk to them about your own conversion experience, discussing often what Jesus did for us, and reading children's books to them about what being a Christian really means.

*Always be available to answer their questions and pray with them, knowing that you are planting seeds of hope everyday.

Many children, who have been brought up in church and on God's Word, will have a "head knowledge" of salvation, sooner than a "heart knowledge." By that I mean that many children may be able to answer all the right questions quite efficiently and yet not be ready to enter into a personal relationship with Jesus. How can we as parents know when our child is ready to commit his heart to Christ?

*Does your child approach you often on the subject?

*Does your child seem more emotional when talking about salvation?

*Is there urgency in their voices as they question others about salvation?

*Are the questions deeper, more personal than previously?

*Is there an overall greater interest in spiritual concerns?

While these are guidelines, always remember to depend on your own knowledge of your child, his maturity level, conceptual ability, and the Holy Spirit's nudges. Just as every child matures at different times, each child will reach a time of accountability before the Lord at different times. There are signs that tell us a child may be ready for salvation, and so too there are signs to watch for that tell us our child is not quite ready.

*Does he lose attention (focus) during conversations relating to the topic?

*Is he quickly ready to move on to other subjects or does he want to play more than finish a discussion on salvation?

*Are his answers to basic questions unclear, or even unsure?

*Does he seem more interested in "getting baptized" because a sibling or friend recently did so or perhaps because it looks fun? A few questions from you could soon allow you to discover the answer to that.

As important as salvation is, as parents, we must remember that it is the Holy Spirit who convicts, preparing hearts for Jesus. We should resist the urge to push our child into this decision. At times we may begin to feel that our child is the only one left from our circle of friends who hasn't made a profession of faith, which may result in "panic" or guilt. By pushing our child into a premature decision for Christ, we rush ahead of the Lord's work, possibly not realizing until much later that what occurred was out of God's timing.

However, if you feel fairly confident that your child has reached a point of being accountable before the Lord, the next step would be to engage in meaningful conversation concerning his desire for salvation by asking poignant questions. Outlined below is a sampling of what your questions might target:

1. Why do you want to ask Jesus into your heart?
2. What does being a Christian mean to you?
3. Why do you think Jesus died on the cross?
4. What is SIN?
5. Who do you believe that Jesus is?
6. Do you believe that Jesus died for your sins and that God raised Him from the dead?

7. How can someone live forever with Jesus in heaven?

Your child should be able to answer these basic questions confidently with no assistance from you. Though the words chosen to explain an answer may sound quite young, if the heart of the answer is right, don't worry if theological wording is not used. If the answers seem ambiguous however, it is a strong indication that they are not quite ready and need more time before making such a commitment.

If all the answers are accurate and displaying a child-like faith, you can feel certain that your child is ready to receive Jesus as Lord and Savior. We know from scripture that no one comes to an understanding of God without being led by the Spirit to do so. Therefore, we must believe that "now" is the time of salvation. Scripture references are provided below to read with your child as you discuss salvation. You can read aloud what has been written in story form if that is more comfortable for you, or you can follow your own discussion using the verses as a reference tool.

*We are all SINNERS and have done things that hurt God. Rom. 3:23

*We deserve to be PUNISHED for all the things we have done that have hurt God. Rom. 6:23

*Jesus loved us so much, even way back then, that He took away our punishment when He died on the cross. He is our ONLY WAY to heaven and to God. John 14:6; John 3:16

*Since Jesus is our only way to God, that means we can't save ourselves or get to heaven by being good or doing any thing else. Going to church can't even save us from the punishment that we deserve. Only by "FAITH," or trusting and believing in Jesus as God's son can we be saved. That doesn't cost anything, not even part of your allowance. It's completely FREE!!

Ephesians 2:8–9, Rom. 6:23

*God wants EVERYONE to be saved and to be with Him forever. John 6:40

*We all do wrong things everyday. Those wrong things are called sins and they keep us away from God. We can be forgiven for those sins, but we have to CONFESS our sins to God (that means to admit that we have done things that we shouldn't have done. Things that have made God very sad.) Matt. 10:32

*We need FORGIVENESS for all the sins we have done and all the ones we still might do. Even the accidental ones still need forgiveness. Because Jesus died on the cross, we can have forgiveness if we just ask God for it. He wants to forgive us! 1 John 1:9

*The Bible also tells us that if we REPENT (that means that we are really, really sorry for what we have done and then do a U-turn, and try to start acting in a different way, a way God would want us to act), God will forgive us of all our sins. Acts 3:19.

We know we have sinned, and we know that Jesus wants to forgive us for our sins. Now all you need to do is to PRAY. Talk to God about your sins and your desire to change. Tell Him how much you want to live with Him forever and make Him happy. Talk to God just like you would talk to your best friend, or your own dad. Invite Him into your life, your heart, just like you would ask your friend to come over to your house and play. It's that simple! He loves you. He wants to forgive you. He wants you to live with Him in heaven someday (John 14:3).

* *Optional prayer: Dear God, I know that I have done many things that have hurt you. I know that those things keep me from being with you. I believe that Jesus is your son and that He died on the cross and was raised from the dead just so I can have forgiveness of all my sins. I want to live for you now, Jesus, and turn away from sinning. Will you come into my heart and forgive me of my sins? I want you to be in charge of my life. Thank you for loving me so much that you want to save me. Amen*

After you pray, you can know for certain that you have ETERNAL LIFE because in Romans 10:13, and Luke 10:20 we are told that whoever calls on Jesus will be saved. And God doesn't lie. You are now a child of the KING! You are a child of God! (John 1:12) Isn't that cool?!

So what's next? Is that all there is to it? Well, almost, but there are still some very important things to do. One is to be BAPTIZED, and the other is to become part of a church family. (Acts 2:41) Jesus was baptized too, and if He was, then it must be *very, very* important. Going to church keeps us learning more and more about Jesus and His love for us. It keeps us near other people who believe in God just like we do. Christian friends can really help us out a lot when we are sad, angry, or even happy.

We also need to try to read the Bible everyday. It is God's special letter He wrote just to us. Some things may be hard to understand, but God will help you as you grow to understand more and more about Him and about the Bible. Ask your parents, your teacher, or your pastor if you get really confused about something.

Finally, we need to pray everyday. God has many names, so it doesn't matter what you call Him: Father, God, Jesus, Lord, Heavenly Father, etc . . . He just wants to hear from you. He also will have special things to say to you too. Just talk to Him like you do your friend, telling Him about your day, your other friends, your pets, your tests at school, or your soccer game. It doesn't matter what you say to Him. Prayer is just talking to God. You don't have to use fancy words or pray very long either. Just be yourself with Him. And, when you do sin, make sure to go straight to God, confessing your sin and asking for His forgiveness. That way you will be sure to keep your relationship with Him strong.

Welcome to the family of God! Remember how much God loves you and tell Him "thank you" often for saving you from your sin. Then tell others about the wonderful miracle of salvation. (Matthew 28:19–20)

Books of the Old and New Testament

Old Testament Books

Genesis

Exodus

Leviticus

Numbers

Deuteronomy

Joshua

Judges

Ruth

I Samuel

II Samuel

I Kings

II Kings

I Chronicles

II Chronicles

Ezra

Nehemiah

Esther

Job

Psalms

Proverbs

Ecclesiastes

Song of Solomon

Isaiah

Jeremiah

Lamentations

Ezekiel

Daniel

Hosea

Joel

Amos

Obadiah

Jonah

Micah

Nahum

Habakkuk

Zephaniah

Haggai

Zechariah

Malachi

New Testament Books

Matthew	
Mark	I Timothy
Luke	II Timothy
John	Titus
Acts	Philemon
Romans	Hebrews
I Corinthians	James
II Corinthians	I Peter
Galatians	II Peter
Ephesians	I John
Philippians	II John
Colossians	III John
I Thessalonians	Jude
II Thessalonians	Revelation

The Seven Days of Creation

Day Count	God Created	We Call It...	Scripture Verse
Day 1	Light	Day and Night	Gen. 1:3
Day 2	Expanse Between the Waters	The Sky	Gen. 1:7
Day 3	a. Dry Ground b. Vegetation	a. Land and Sea b. Plants and Trees	Gen. 1:9
Day 4	Lights in the Sky	The Sun, Moon and Stars	Gen. 1:14
Day 5	Every Living Thing in the Sea and Air	All the Fish and All the Birds	Gen. 1:21
Day 6	a. Living Creatures on Land b. Man c. Green Plants for Food	a. Animals, Reptiles and Insects b. Adam c. Fruits and Vegetables	a. Gen. 1:24 b. Gen. 1:26 c. Gen. 1:30
Day 7	Rest	Sunday	Gen. 2:2

The 23rd Psalm

The LORD is my shepherd, I shall not be in want. He makes me lie down in green pastures, he leads me beside quiet waters, he restores my soul. He guides me in paths of righteousness for his name's sake. Even though I walk through the valley of the shadow of death, I will fear no evil, for you are with me; your rod and your staff, they comfort me.

You prepare a table before me in the presence of my enemies. You anoint my head with oil; my cup overflows. Surely goodness and love will follow me all the days of my life, and I will dwell in the house of the LORD forever.

(Psalm 23:1-6; NIV)

The LORD is my shepherd; I shall not want. He maketh me to lie down in green pastures: He leadeth me beside the still waters. He restoreth my soul: He leadeth me in the paths of righteousness for his name's sake. Yea, though I walk through the valley of the shadow of death, I will fear no evil: for thou art with me; thy rod and thy staff they comfort me.

Thou preparest a table before me in the presence of mine enemies: thou anointest my head with oil; my cup runneth over. Surely goodness and mercy shall follow me all the days of my life: and I will dwell in the house of the LORD for ever.

(Psalm 23:1-6; KJV)

The Twelve Disciples of Jesus

Luke 6:13-16

Simon (whom He named Peter)

Andrew, Simon's brother

James

John

Philip

Bartholomew

Matthew

Thomas

James (son of Alphaeus)

Simon (the Zealot)

Judas (son of James)

Judas Iscariot, who betrayed Jesus

AND

Matthias

(After Judas Iscariot died, the remaining eleven Disciples
chose Matthias to replace him. Acts 1:26)

The Lord's Prayer

Our Father, which art in heaven, Hallowed be thy name. Thy kingdom come. Thy will be done in earth, as it is in heaven. Give us this day our daily bread. And forgive us our debts, as we forgive our debtors. And lead us not into temptation, but deliver us from evil: For thine is the kingdom, and the power, and the glory, for ever. Amen.

(Matthew 6:9-13; KJV)

The Golden Rule

Therefore, however you want people to treat you, so treat them, for this is the Law and the Prophets.

(Matthew 7:12; NAS)

The Greatest Commandment

Jesus replied: "'Love the Lord your God with all your heart and with all your soul and with all your mind.' This is the first and greatest commandment. And the second is like it: 'Love your neighbor as yourself.'"

(Matthew 22:37-39; NIV)

The Great Commission

Therefore go and make disciples of all nations, baptizing them in the name of the Father and of the Son and of the Holy Spirit, and teaching them to obey everything I have commanded you. And surely I am with you always, to the very end of the age.

(Matthew 28:19-20; NIV)

The Fruit of the Spirit

But the fruit of the Spirit is:

Love

Joy

Peace

Patience

Kindness

Goodness

Gentleness

Faithfulness

Self-Control

Against such things there is no law.

Galatians 5:22–23

The Love Chapter

Love is patient, love is kind. It does not envy, it does not boast, it is not proud. It is not rude, it is not self-seeking, it is not easily angered, it keeps no record of wrongs. Love does not delight in evil but rejoices with the truth. It always protects, always trusts, always hopes, always perseveres.

Love never fails . . . And now these three remain: faith, hope and love. But the greatest of these is love. (1 Corinthians 13:4-8;13 NIV)

Love Is:	Love Is Not:
Patient	Envious
Kind	Boastful
Rejoices with the Truth	Proud
Protects	Rude
Hopes	Selfish
Perseveres	Angry
Never Fails	
Does not keep count of "wrongs"	
Does not delight in evil	

The Roman's Road

You must recognize that you are a sinner and need a relationship with Jesus:

"For all have sinned and fall short of the glory of God." (Romans 3:23)

"For the wages of sin is death, but the gift of God is eternal life in Christ Jesus our Lord."

(Romans 6:23)

"But God demonstrates his own love for us in this: While we were still sinners, Christ died for us." (Romans 5:8)

You must confess your sins and repent:

"That if you confess with your mouth, "Jesus is Lord," and believe in your heart that God raised him from the dead, you will be saved. (Romans 10:9)

Ask Jesus to save you by His grace:

"Everyone who calls on the name of the Lord will be saved." (Romans 10:13)

Turn your life over to Jesus and let Him be Lord.

Grace: God *giving blessings* to us that we don't deserve, because of His Love for us.

Mercy: God *withholding* punishment that we do deserve, because of His Love for us.

The Armor of God

Therefore put on the full armor of God, so that when the day of evil comes, you may be able to stand your ground . . . Stand firm then, with the belt of truth buckled around your waist, with the breastplate of righteousness in place, and with your feet fitted with the readiness that comes from the gospel of peace.

In addition to all this, take up the shield of faith, with which you can extinguish all the flaming arrows of the evil one. Take the helmet of salvation and the sword of the Spirit, which is the word of God.

And pray in the Spirit on all occasions with all kinds of prayers and requests. With this in mind, be alert and always keep on praying for all the saints. (Ephesians 6:13-18; NIV)

Christian's Godly Armor		
Belt	Truth	Waist
Breastplate	Righteousness	Chest
Shoes	Peace	Feet
Shield	Faith	"All"
Helmet	Salvation	Head (Knowledge)
Sword (God's Word)	Spirit	Defensive Tool
Prayer	Spirit	On All Occasions (Be Alert)

Monthly and Thematic Summary

January- God's Wonderful Creation

The month of January will be concentrating on the wonderful aspects of God's creation. The devotionals will guide boys and girls to see God as the majestic ruler, creator and "owner" over everything in the world. It will also encourage children through practical application ways they can take care of God's world.

Week 1- Everything Belongs to God

Theme: The devotional thought will encourage boys and girls to take care of God's world, and through practical suggestions show them ways they can do so.

Memory Verse: Genesis 1:1

References: Psalm 100:3; 4:8

Week 2- Made in His Image

Theme: This week will be showing the boys and girls how special they are since they are created by God and made in His image. It will further examine what it means to be created in the image of God.

Memory Verse: Genesis 1: 27

References: Genesis 5:1–2; Psalm 100:3; Romans14:8; 1 Corinthians 3:16

Week 3- Wonderfully Made

Theme: Self- Esteem. Boys and girls will learn the value of accepting themselves as God has designed them and why they should love themselves just as they are. Even very young children enjoy hearing about being created and how much they are loved.

Memory Verse: Psalm 139:14

References: Psalm 1:36; Isaiah 43:4; Philippians 1:6; James 1:17

Week 4- Created Equal

Theme: Equality among others. This week will teach children that because everyone is created equal in God's eyes, we ought also treat others with the love and respect God shows to us, showing no favoritism. Since God made us all different, we should learn to appreciate the differences found in others, rather than reject them for those differences.

Memory Verse: Romans 10:12

References: Genesis 11: 1–9; Proverbs 27:2; Matthew 7:1,12; Matthew 22: 39; 2 Corinthians 12:9; James 2:1; Philippians 2:3

February- Basketful of Fruit

The month of February traditionally centers on love, which happens to be one of the fruits listed as part of the Fruit of the Spirit. What a perfect opportunity to express to our children what the Fruit of the Spirit is, where it comes from and why it is important in a believer's life. The month of February will expound upon the Fruit of the Spirit in terms children will better understand.

Week 1- Fruit of the Spirit

Theme: An overview of the Fruit of the Spirit, what it means and why it needs to be evident in a Christian's life.

Memory Verse: Galatians 5:22-23

References: Matthew 7:20; John 15:16; Colossians 3:12–14

Week 2- What is Love?

Theme: Emphasizing the fruit of love, its part in a believer's life and why it is important, this week will explain that love is much more than just saying words and liking something.

Memory Verse: 1 Corinthians 13:13

References: Matthew 5:44; John 13:34- 35; I Corinthians 13:4; I Corinthians 13:8; I Peter 4:8

Week 3- Kindest Attitude

Theme: The sweet fruit of Kindness and how it relates to relationships that children form will be the background to this week's devotional.

Memory Verse: Ephesians 4:32

References: Matthew 7:12; John 15:17; Galatians 6:10; I Thessalonians 5:15

Week 4- Self-Controlled, not Remote Controlled

Theme: Learning to control impulses, including anger, this week's study will relate the importance of thinking before acting, and being in control of one's own emotions.

Memory Verse: I Peter 5:8

References: Psalm 29:11; 1 Peter 1:13;1 Peter 4:7

March- More Than Just the Easter Bunny

With Easter occurring oftentimes during the month of March, this unit will be highlighting the true meaning of Easter and what salvation is.

Week 1- What Is Sin?

Theme: The first week discusses sin, what it is, and the fact that we are all sinners, even little children.

Memory Verse: Romans 5:8

References: Isaiah 59:2; Romans 3:23; Romans 6:23; James 4:17

Week 2- Mercy Me!

Theme: Grace and Mercy will be explained and discussed.

Memory Verse: Ephesians 2:8-9

References: Romans 8 34- 35; I Peter 1:3- 4; Titus 2:11

Week 3- Forgive Me, Forgive Me Not

Theme: Forgiveness . . . children will see the importance of for-giveness, even when they don't feel like forgiving someone.

Memory Verse: I John 1:9

References: Psalm 103:12; John 3:16; I Timothy 1:15; I Timothy 2:4- 5; I John 4:10–11

Week 4- New Life on the Farm

Theme: New Life through Jesus will be explained through an analogy of baby animals being born on a farm.

Memory Verse: 2 Corinthians 5:17

References: Isaiah 65:17; Matthew 28:5- 7; Mark 16:6; John 20:31; I Corinthians15:52; I Thessalonians 4:13–18; I Peter 1:23; Revelation 3:20

April- Qualities of a Christian

After learning about salvation and receiving Christ, learning what a Christian "looks" like and acts like is the next step in Christian growth. Although many children are too young to have accepted Jesus as Lord and Savior, it is never too early to teach them *how* a Christian should behave.

Week 1- Light Your World

Theme: Being light in a dark world. It will show in simple terms how a follower of Jesus should "shine" in the world/community where they live through their good works and kind deeds.

Memory Verse: Matthew 5:16

References: Matthew 5:14; John 14:15; I Thessalonians 4:7

Week 2- Careful Conduct

Theme: Learning to be careful in both words and action is part of living the way Jesus wants us to live.

Memory Verse: James 1:22

References: Proverbs15:1; Proverbs 15:23; I Colossians 3:23–24; I Thessalonians 4:11–12

Week 3- Bold Witness for Christ

Theme: Telling others about Christ and being courageous in ones stand for Jesus is the theme for this week.

Memory Verse: Matthew 28:19-20

References: Matthew 10:32; Romans 1:16; 2 Timothy 1:12; I Peter 1:15

Week 4- Loving our Enemies

Theme: Learning about a forgiving spirit even to those who are our enemies. When, why, and how to forgive will be expressed in this chapter.

Memory Verse: Matthew 6:14-15

References: Matthew 5:23- 24; Matthew 18:21- 22; Ephesians 4:32; Colossians 3:13

May– Who is God?

This unit's theme will be concentrating on the triune God and His attributes. Though children will not be able to comprehend the whole concept of the Trinity, through a week by week "study" they will more clearly understand each role of God in relation to the Trinity.

Week 1- God, the Father

Theme: Week one is emphasizing the attributes of God as our Heavenly Father.

Memory Verse: Isaiah 46:9

References: Psalm 46:10a; Isaiah 46:9; Matthew 7:9–12; I Peter 1:15; I John 4:8; Revelation 1:8

Week 2- God, the Son

Theme: Learning more about Jesus, God's son, children will be given two verses for memory, though one may be sufficient.

Memory Verse: John 14:6; Hebrews 1:3

References: Matthew 1:21,23; John 1:1–4; John 10; John 11:25; Acts 4:12; 2 Corinthians 5:21; Philippians 2:6- 11; Colossians 1:15- 20; Colossians 2:9; Hebrews 13:8; Revelation 1:13–7

Week 3- God, the Holy Spirit

Theme: Children will learn the role of the Holy Spirit in the life of Christians

Memory Verse: John 14:26

References: John 14:15- 16; Romans 8:26; I Corinthians 3:16; Galatians 5:22–25 Ephesians1:13–14; Ephesians 4:30

Week 4- The Many Qualities of God

Theme: Attributes of God rounds out the unit on "Who is God?" Attributes such as His holiness, graciousness, compassion, and love are brought to life as the children are led to a better understanding of the many qualities of God

Memory Verse: 1 Peter 1:15

References: Joshua 1:5; Psalm 103:8–13,17; Psalm 107:1; Isaiah 9:6; I Peter 5:7; I John 4:8

June- Respecting Others

Having just honored Mother's Day and with Father's Day fast approaching, learning proper respect for others seems the natural choice for the month of June. This month will be divided into various groups of people that we are admonished to respect.

Week 1- Respecting Parents

Theme: Children will see what God has to say about respecting parents, the blessing that follows, and what respect is NOT.

Memory Verse: Ephesians 6:1

References: Exodus 20:12; Leviticus 19:3

Week 2- Respecting Authority

Theme: Regardless of whom it is or what our feelings are towards the figure in authority, children will see the importance of learning to respect everyone, even those with whom we disagree.

Memory Verse: Romans13:1

References: I Peter 2:17; I Peter 2:13; Titus 3:1- 2

Week 3- Respecting Your Elders

Theme: Though all young children seem to love their grand-parents, sometimes they forget the importance of respecting the older generation. Through this week's theme, they will be shown the value God has placed on respect for the elderly

Memory Verse: Leviticus 19:32

References: Romans 13:1- 5; I Thessalonians 5:12–13; Hebrews 13:17

Week 4- Respecting Your Peers

Theme: Showing respect towards kids their own age is some-times the hardest group to learn to respect. Through this study children will learn different ways of showing respect towards peers by listening, supporting, not making fun, and accepting those that are different.

Memory Verse: I Peter 2:17

References: Romans 12:10; Romans 14:1; Romans 14:13; Romans 15:7; I Thessalonians 5:12- 13; James 2:1

July- Christian Basics . . . What, Why and How?

Children are filled with a heart full of questions. The more they learn, the more they seem to inquire. As they grow in their young faith, many begin to wonder "why" to many aspects of the faith. Through this unit of study, children will have many of their questions answered on the basics of the Christian life.

Week 1- Does God Hear Me When I Pray?

Theme: As children are taught to pray, many may wonder why, how and when they should pray. This week's study will attempt to answer their many questions relating to prayer.

Memory Verse: Matthew 7:7–8

References: Psalm 139: 23- 24; Philippians 4:19; I John 5:14

Week 2- What is the Bible?

Theme: Children will learn why the Bible is valued, why memorizing scripture is important, and how the Bible got its existence.

Memory Verse: Psalm 119:105; Psalm 119:11

References: Proverbs 8:10; Isaiah 40:8; Isaiah 55:11–12; Ephesians 6:10- 11; 2 Timothy 3:16-17; Hebrews 4:12

Week 3- Church . . . Again?

Theme: Church attendance and what church is all about will be the focus for week three

Memory Verse: Psalm 122:1

References: Ephesians 10:25–26; Hebrews 10:25

Week 4- What is Faith?

Theme: Probably one of the most difficult aspects of the Christian life is in explaining to children what living by **faith** is all about. Maybe that is because as adults we struggle with it so much ourselves. Though children can never be expected to fully comprehend the depths of faith witnessed in God's Word, through this week's devotion, they will more clearly understand what faith is and its role in the Christian life.

Memory Verse: Hebrews 11: 6

References: Proverbs 3:5; Hebrews 11:1; Romans 5:1; 2 Corinthians 5:7; James 2:26

August- Fantastic Friendships

Children of all ages love to play with friends. As they near school age however, choosing friends becomes more of a concern for parents. Many children don't know how to find good friends, or what constitutes a good friend. Throughout this month, they will see the importance of choosing friends wisely.

Week 1- Choosing Friends

Theme: Young children will learn the value of choosing wholesome, fun friends as they follow through this week's theme.

Memory Verse: James 4:4

References: Proverbs 17:17; Proverbs 18:24; I Corinthians 15:33; 2 Corinthians 6:14; Hebrews 10:24

Week 2- Learning to Compromise

Theme: As friends are made, learning to compromise becomes increasingly important. Children will gain insight into what compromise is all about and why it is important in maintaining relationships with others.

Memory Verse: 2 Timothy 2:23–24

References: Romans 12:16; Romans 14:19; Romans 15:5; 2 Timothy 2:14,16; Titus 3:9

Week 3- Do Unto Others As. . . . ?

Theme: The Golden Rule. Relationships involve many facets, but the way we *treat* others is one of the most important. Children discover early how they want to be treated and how to express those desires but learning how to treat others is not as easy.

Memory Verse: Matthew 7:12

References: Matthew 5:44; Matthew 22:39; John 13:34; Romans 12:17–18; Romans14:13,19; Romans15:1–2, 7

Week 4- Temptation/Strength

Theme: Peer pressure doesn't wait until the teenage years to strike. Even preschoolers are faced with pressure every day to do what is wrong as opposed to what they know as right. Whether it be to lie, steal or disobey authority, children can learn how to resist the temptation to do what appears appealing at the moment with grace and strength.

Memory Verse: 2 Chronicles 19:11; James 4:7–8a

References: Acts 5:29; Hebrews 2:18; I Corinthians 10:12- 14; I Corinthians 15:58; 2 Timothy 2:19; I John 4:4

September- Building Strong Values

Teaching children about the importance of solid values is challenging today in a world where they are so overlooked for other less important ideals. Through this month's theme children will learn the importance of integrity and strong moral values.

Week 1- Always Do Your Best

Theme: Doing ones best regardless of the cost is the theme for the first week.

Memory Verse: Colossians 3:23

References: Proverbs 6:10–11; Proverbs 10:4; Proverbs 16:3; Hebrews 10:34–35; I Thessalonians 4:11–12; I Thessalonians 5:12; 2 Timothy 2:15

Week 2- Being Responsible

Theme: Learning to be responsible and developing strong work ethics, responsibility can never be overemphasized. Whether it be for ones actions or for a job, children must learn early on reasonable responsibility in a variety of situations.

Memory Verse: Galatians 6:4–5

References: Matthew 12:37; 1 Corinthians 7:24; Hebrews 4:13

Week 3- Honesty is the Best Policy

Theme: Teaching children to be honest in all areas of life, with grace and tact, is a tough challenge. Learning what the Bible has to say about lying and the importance of honesty will help assist parents and their children as they face temptation.

Memory Verse: Psalm 34:13–14

References: Leviticus19:11; Proverbs 6:17; John 8:44; Ephesians 4:29; Colossians 3:9

Week 4- True to Yourself

Theme: Standing for what is right and for who they are regardless of popularity is a tough challenge for children, but through the verse and story this week, they will have a better understanding of what it means to be "true to yourself."

Memory Verse: 1 Corinthians 15:58

References: Romans 1:16; I Corinthians 16:13; 2 Timothy 1:12

October- Those Crazy Feelings

God has placed within each person a range of emotions to experience and express. Sometimes however, children repress certain feelings assuming they are "bad". Through the month of October, children will learn that all feelings are a gift of God, designed for a special purpose. Each week will highlight a different emotion for discussion.

Week 1- I've Got the Joy, Joy, Joy, Joy!

Theme: Week one will talk about happy feelings and the difference between "joy" and "happiness".

Memory Verse: Proverbs 15:13

References: Ecclesiastes 3:1, 4; Psalm 28:7; Psalm 126; Proverbs 17:22; Isaiah 55:12; John 10:10; Philippians 4:1; I Thessalonians 5:16

Week 2- No S'more Tears

Theme: Children need to be reminded of the presence of God in their lives at all times, and know that He can't be scared away by their feelings. Sadness is a natural part of life, yet God is there to comfort and hold us close to His heart as we experience heartbreak.

Memory Verse: Psalm 34:18

References: Psalm 34:15; Isaiah 61:1–2; Luke 6:21*b*, Hebrews 12:3

Week 3-Angry Words, Hurtful Heart

Theme: Being angry is okay, but what we do in our anger can lead to sin.

Memory Verse: Psalm 4:4

References: Proverbs 15:1; Psalm 29:11; Psalm 29:22; Ephesians 4:26- 27; I Peter 5:8

Week 4- I Will Fear No Evil

Theme: Week four ties in with Halloween and discusses with children the feelings of fear. God doesn't want us to live life in fear and anxiety. Many things abound today to cause fear and worry in a child's life, but in learning what scripture has to say about fear, they will be better equipped to handle the "scary" things of life.

Memory Verse: 2 Timothy 1:7

References: Joshua 1:5, 6,7,9; Psalm 27:1; Isaiah 40:31; Psalm 56:3; Matthew 6:34; 2 Corinthians 12:9; I Peter 5:7; I John 4:4,18

November- Hip, Hip, Hooray! It's Thanksgiving Day

Throughout this month, each week will concentrate on a different reason to celebrate the holiday and different ways we can go about expressing our gratitude.

Week 1- Praise Him, Praise Him!

Theme: Learning what praise is, how to praise God, and when to praise Him is the theme for this week

Memory Verse: Psalm 118: 24

References: Psalm 8:1; Psalm 66; Psalm 92; Psalm 100:1- 5; Psalm 107:1

Week 2- Answered Prayer

Theme: The magnificent acts that God has done, who He is, and what He has given to us should bring forth triumphant thankfulness within our hearts at all times. This week will look at what we have been given and why we should offer thanks to God spontaneously as well as on a regular basis, not just at the dinner table.

Memory Verse: Psalm 107:1

References: Psalm 118:24; Corinthians15:57; Philippians 1:3; James 1:17

Week 3- God's Great Guidance

Theme: Children will learn of God's leadership and guidance in all areas of life throughout the course of week three. As children face uncertain situations or need wisdom in making decisions, they can be sure of guidance of Romans a loving father.

Memory Verse: Psalm 32:8

References: Psalm 23:2; Psalm 25:9; Psalm 32:8; Proverbs 3:5-6; 2 Corinthians 2:14

Week 4- An Attitude of Gratitude

Theme: All parents desire their children to appreciate what they have been given. Through week four, children will learn the importance of having a grateful attitude and ways to demonstrate thankfulness.

Memory Verse: Ephesians 5:19–20

References: Psalm 8:9; Psalm 9:1- 2; Psalm 28:7*b;* Psalm 95:1-2; Ephesians 5:18; Colossians. 3:16

December- Giving From the Heart

December, along with Christmas, has long been associated with gift giving. Children of all ages thrill at the thought of being the recipient of so many beautifully wrapped packages awaiting them on Christmas morning. But as Christian parents, we long for our children to understand the deeper meaning of the season. All parents desire their children to appreciate what they have and to discover the greater joy found in giving rather than receiving. Each devotional this month will focus on giving and being thankful for what we already have.

Week 1- Sacrificial Giving

Theme: Children will learn what tithing is, why the tithe is important, and what God has in store for those who do tithe.

Memory Verse: Malachi 3:10

References: Proverbs 3:9

Week 2- Joyful Givers

Theme: Along with tithing, children need to learn the value and pleasure of giving with a cheerful spirit. Week two targets giving cheerfully, as well as sacrificially.

Memory Verse: 2 Corinthians 9:7

References: Luke 6:38; Acts 20:35; 2 Corinthians 8:7,12

Week 3- Sharing from the Heart

Theme: When we learn to hold loosely to the things of this world and value spiritual ideals more, giving to those in need becomes less of a burden and much more of a joy. By holding loosely to earthly possessions, we tend not to count the cost of what has been given away. Children are taught to "share" from the earliest days of life, but through the devotion this week, they will learn the deeper meaning of sharing cheerfully, whether it's their favorite toys, their time, or even sharing of their talents.

Memory Verse: Matthew 6:19–21

References: Matthew 6:3- 4; Luke 6: 38; Acts 20:35; Romans 12:6- 8; Philippians 4:19; I Peter 4:10

Week 4- The Greatest Gift

Theme: No matter what we give to others, no matter how much it may cost us to help another in need, we can never out give God and what He has done through the gift of His son Jesus Christ. Week four focuses on the theme of **Jesus' birth**, the greatest gift ever given.

Memory Verse: Luke 2:10–11

References: Isaiah 9:6; Matthew 1:21

"Wow," shouted Timmy, "these mountains are huge! They look like giant roller coasters."

"And look at the pretty clouds, too," squealed an all too excited Whitney. They're so fluffy and white. I think they look like giant marshmallows floating on water." Four year old Whitney couldn't help thinking about her favorite snack-marshmallows!

As six year old Timmy skipped rocks over the mountain stream, he thought about what a wonderful vacation this was turning out to be. He was sorry he had complained so much about going to the mountains instead of the amusement park.

The sky-scraping trees, the cool summer stream, the lush green grass . . . it was all too much for Timmy and Whitney. They had never seen so much color in one place before.

"Hey, kids, come over here and look at this," Dad whispered softly to his two wide-eyed youngsters.

As they quietly approached, they spied a red squirrel scurrying on the ground, looking for food. "Did you know that God takes care of that squirrel just like He takes care of you? He provides food for the squirrel and all the other wildlife hiding among the trees. God created everything you see out here and He takes good care of His creations everyday," Dad told them.

"How does He do that, Dad?" Timmy wanted to know all about this beautiful world he was looking at.

"God provides food for the animals through nature. Trees, plants, and other living things help supply the animals with the food and shelter that they need to survive. The rain and sun also help nourish life outdoors. But, God wants us to help Him too. He wants us to help Him take care of all that we see.

After all, since He gave it to us to enjoy, don't you think one way we could say 'thank you' is by taking care of it?"

"Well how can we help God? Isn't He the biggest of all? He doesn't need our help does he?"

"That's a very good question Whitney," Mom answered. "Yes, God is the 'biggest' of all, but He still wants us to help Him. It shows Him how much we care. One way we can show God how much we care is by always throwing our trash in a trash can when we are finished with it. By not littering, we are helping to keep God's world looking pretty. Our trash can kill the grass that animals need for food. It can also kill the animals in the ponds and streams like this one here. If we don't take care of it now, we won't have places like this to enjoy anymore. There are lots of ways we can help take care of God's world. Why don't we think together of some other ways that we can show God how much we love His beautiful world.

"That's a good idea Mommy," Whitney said and smiled as she gently knelt to smell a pretty flower.

Timmy had to agree as he carefully searched for another small stone to toss into the babbling stream.

"Bloo-wip! Bloo-wip!" laughed the stones as they skidded across the surface of the water.

"Hey, Dad, can we come back here again sometime? This is a cool vacation."

Let's Think About Creation

Have you ever been to the mountains before?

Where is your favorite place to be?

What are some ways that you could help Timmy and Whitney take care of God's world?

As you read about many of God's creations this month, think about ways that you can show God how much you appreciate what He has made.

Week One–Everything Belongs to God

Genesis 1:1
In the beginning God created the heavens and the earth. (NIV)

In the beginning God created the heavens and the earth. (KJV)

Have you ever wondered who made the tall trees, the mountains, or the big wavy ocean? The Bible tells us that God was the one who made all these things. A long, long, *long* time ago, when the world was very dark, before you or even your grandparents were born, God created the world and everything in it. WOW! That's a lot of work, isn't it? He made the heavens and the earth first, and then He filled it with all sorts of great things like the ocean, the twinkling stars, and even the wild animals. After He finished His work, He looked around at all He had accomplished and said it was, "very good." He was proud of His creation!

Since God was the one who came up with the idea, and since He is the one who did all the work, everything in this world belongs to our heavenly Father. It isn't ours at all. In a way, you might say that God has "loaned" it to us for a while to enjoy and to remind us of Him. But, it is still His.

Have you ever made something really, really special like a pretty picture with bright markers, or a model rocket, or a great design out of blocks? How did it make you feel when you stood back and saw your work? If someone accidentally broke it or threw it away, how do you think you would feel then? You might feel a little angry at the person who was careless with your special project. After all, you did make it all by yourself and you were proud of the hard work that went into making it. You might be especially hurt if you made it for someone you cared about very much and then they threw it away.

That's exactly how God feels. He loves us so much that He has given us all the pretty things we see outside everyday. He expects us to take care of them though. Imagine how hurt He must feel when He sees trash in His parks or streets or rivers. When He sees animals being hurt or abandoned, and people carelessly setting fire to forests, He must feel very sad. God wants us to be responsible for the world around us. Everything belongs to God, but we must take good care of it for Him.

Let's Talk About the Story

Who created (made) the world?

According to the memory verse, what two things did God make first?

Can you think of three things that God made for you to enjoy?

Which is your favorite?

It's easy to tell someone thank you for a nice gift, but how can you *show* God that you appreciate what He has created?

This week as you play outside, think of God and what He has made for us. Remember to pick up your trash, too. Maybe you could even pick up someone else's trash and throw it away. Whatever you do, do your best to keep God's world clean and looking pretty.

Prayer

Dear Father,

Thank you so much for making the heavens and the earth. Thank you for letting us enjoy so many nice things everyday. Forgive us for not always being careful with our trash, and help us to do better at keeping your world clean. We love you, God. Amen

Family Activity

This week, schedule time when the whole family can go outside and pick up trash together. You'll need a large trash bag and maybe some smaller plastic grocery bags for the kids to carry around. As you pick up trash, talk about the value of cleaning up the area where you live. Remind the kids that everything they see belongs to God and we must be very careful with someone else's belongings.

Reference Verses: Psalm 100:3; Romans 14:8

Week Two—Made in His Image

Genesis 1:27

So God created man in his own image,* in the image of God he created him; male and female he created them. (NIV)

So God created man in his own image,* in the image of God created he him; male and female created he them. (KJV)

Blake and Hannah were excited. Today their mom would be coming home from the hospital with their new baby brother, Christopher. They could hardly wait!

They got to see him after he was born, but they couldn't hold him. Now, they could touch him, kiss him, and hold him all they wanted.

"Blake, hurry now. Your mom and dad will be home soon,"Grandma said from the kitchen.

Blake hurried to clean his room. He didn't want to miss one moment of this special occasion.

The rumble of the garage door soon signaled to all in the house that they were finally home. As the hours passed, Blake and Hannah could hardly leave baby Christopher's side. Dad had noticed how carefully Hannah had been looking at her new baby brother and then looking in a mirror at her own reflection. After watching this repeatedly for several minutes, Dad decided to sit on the floor next to Hannah and find out what she was doing.

"Daddy, why are Christopher's eyes a different color from mine? Isn't he my brother? And where are his freckles? I don't see any on his nose." Three-year-old Hannah wanted to know all about her new baby brother.

"Well, yes, Hannah, Christopher is your brother and he always will be, but he won't look exactly like you. He will look a little like us and a lot like himself. God made both of you special and different from anybody else in this whole world."

"The Bible tells us that God made every boy and girl in His own image. That means that He made you and Blake and Christopher to resemble or act something like Him. We don't know what God looks like; no one has ever seen Him. But we do know that something about us reminds God of Himself. The word "image" means something like a picture of someone else. A picture isn't really a person, but it looks like the person it was made of. One part of us that is like God's image is the part of us that helps us to think and feel. God makes right choices all the time, and since we are made in His image, we too have the ability to make right choices that please God. We also have feelings of anger, sadness, and happiness just like God. We know that God is love so we too have the ability to love, like the love and care you feel towards your new brother. When God made Christopher, He made him in His image. He reminds God of Himself in the way he thinks, acts, and feels. Yet, he will look a little like you, a bit like Blake, and he just might look like me and Mommy too.

"Oh, I think I get it now," Hannah said proudly, "we are all different, but we are all made like God. Like one big family. Can I hold my new brother now? I want to tell him all about his new family."

Let's Talk About the Story

The Bible tells us that we are made in the image of whom? (who are we made like?)

Why do you think God created us like Him?

Since we are created in God's own image, we have the ability to love others and to make what kind of choices?

Do you think God will help you make good choices when you don't know what to do?

Prayer

Dear Father,

Thank you for making (child's name) like yourself. Thank you for making (child's name) so special and like nobody else. Help me as I grow to learn how to make good choices that will always please you. I love you God. Amen

Family Activity

Plan a time this week when you can bring out the family photo albums or baby pictures. Sit together on the floor and talk about the pictures and what was happening when they were made. Remind your children of how special they are because they are made in the image of God, the creator of the heavens and the earth.

References: Genesis 5:1–2, 1 Corinthians 3:16

Week Three–Wonderfully Made

Psalm 139:14

I praise you because I am fearfully and wonderfully made; *
your works are wonderful, I know that full well. (NIV)

I will praise thee; for I am fearfully and wonderfully made: *
marvelous are thy works;
and that my soul knoweth right well. (KJV)

SLAM! The screen door closed with a bang. "It's not fair! Why does Taylor always have to win. He can do everything better than me!" Jon-Michael shouted loud through the tears as he ran upstairs to his room.

Mom followed behind, wanting to see what had caused this latest outburst.

"Jon-Michael, what just happened out there? You two boys were playing so well together."

"It's just Taylor, Mom. He can do everything better than me. I can't do anything right when he's around. I don't ever want to play with him again."

Ten year old Jon-Michael and eight year old Taylor were brothers and often times, the best of friends. But today, something was causing Jon-Michael to feel very different towards his little brother.

"Jon-Michael, what do you mean when you say you can't do anything right when he is around? I've seen you do many things well even when Taylor is here."

"Wrong, Mom. In case you haven't noticed, Taylor does everything better than me. He always beats me when we play basketball, soccer, baseball, you name it; he always wins! I think God must have made a mistake when he made me."

"Jon-Michael, you are partly right. Taylor is a very good athlete. He is a natural when it comes to sports, but that doesn't mean you don't have special gifts and abilities yourself."

"Yeah, like what Mom? Channel-surfing?" Jon-Michael was frustrated. He wanted to feel better, but at the moment all he could focus on was losing.

"You are a natural musician. You have a good ear for music. Think of how easy the piano was for you to learn. Of course, you still have to practice every day, but it is easier for you than it is for Taylor, and you enjoy it so much. You also sing well. You are a great student, and you are quite creative," Mother added as she scanned his room, noticing all the many drawings pinned on his walls. "Jon-Michael, God made you and Taylor very different, but that doesn't mean that Taylor is a better person than you. God made each of us unique. In Psalm 139:14, we are told that we are 'fearfully and wonderfully made.' That means we are all made according to God's perfect design. We are one of God's wonderful works of creation. Remember how God saw all that He had made in the beginning and said that it was very good? That includes you too. God thinks you are wonderful, He loves the way He has created you. He wants you to love yourself too. He wants you to like who He has made you to be.

"But, Mom, why can't I play ball as well as Taylor can? It doesn't seem fair."

"Jon-Michael, I think that if you practiced as hard at ball as you do the piano, you could become much better. Except for winning though and beating Taylor, I don't think ball is very important to you. I know it isn't important to us. What is important is that you are the best you that you can be. You aren't supposed to be like Taylor or anyone else. Find something you are good at and do it well. Then work hard on the other things that you aren't so good at. You'll find you are much happier that way."

Just then Taylor came bouncing up the stairs. "Hey, Jon-Michael, where are you?"

"Oh, hi Taylor, I'm getting ready to practice the piano. I have a recital coming up soon, and I want to be ready for it."

"I don't know how you can play the piano so well Jon-Michael. You're really good at it. That's cool how you can play so fast and all."

"Thanks Taylor. I guess God just made us different, huh?"

Let's Talk About the Story

Why was Jon-Michael so upset?

What does the Bible tell us about what God thinks of us?

Have you ever felt bad because someone else could do something better than you? Tell about that time.

If God loves us just as we are, how should we feel about ourselves?

Tell God how thankful you are for making you special.

Prayer

Dear Father,

Thank you for loving me and making me different from everyone else. Thank you for the things I can do well. I love you God. Amen

Family Activities

Sometime during the week find time to sit down together and let each person tell something special about every other person in the family. Then pray for each person.

References: Psalm 1:36; Isaiah 43:4; Philippians 1:6; James 1:17

Week Four–Created Equal

Romans 10:12
For there is no difference between Jew and Gentile—the same Lord is Lord of all* and richly blesses all who call on him . . . (NIV)

For there is no difference between the Jew and the Greek; for the same Lord over all is rich unto all that call upon him. (KJV)

What do you notice when you look into a big box of crayons? How about when you gaze into the sky at a beautiful rainbow? Do you see many wonderful colors dancing together in a row? Did you know that God made all the colors you see and use everyday? God created color just like He created everything else in the world.

Can you imagine a crayon box with 24 red crayons in it? Or imagine how disappointed you would be if you stepped outside to view the rainbow after a spring rain and discovered the only color appearing in the sky was the color green. Life without different colors would be so boring! That's exactly how people are. The world is kind of like a big crayon box waiting to be opened. God created all different kinds of people. Some have dark hair while some have red. What color of eyes do you have? Are they the same color as everyone else's in your family? God made blue eyes to see the same things that green eyes see. They aren't better or worse, just different. Do you have dark colored skin or are you fair skinned? Does your family speak a different language from other people you know?

No matter what you look like or what language you speak, God made everyone equal. "Equal" means "the same," like when you get the same size birthday cake as your sister, you have "equal" amounts; the same. When God sees you, no matter where you live, He loves you the same as the person from another part of the world. We are not better, or worse, than anyone else because of our eye color, our hair color, the language we speak, or even the clothes that we wear. We are all the same. That's what the Bible means when it says that there is no difference between Jews or Gentiles. He is the same Lord, and He blesses everyone the same when they follow Him, no matter what they look like. In Bible times, Jews and Gentiles didn't like each other very much and they worshiped God in very different ways. They each felt God loved them more than the other. God wanted them to know that He didn't care who they were, He loved and blessed them all the same when they obeyed His teaching.

Do you know someone who is different from you? Maybe he doesn't have nice clothes as you do, or maybe his house isn't as big as yours. Or, perhaps you know someone who must walk differently or who learns in a different way than you do. Maybe you are that person. God wants us to love and respect everyone regardless of how much money they have or how they look. We should never laugh, whisper, or make fun of others in way that would hurt their feelings if they were to hear us. When we show respect to other people that are different from us, we are showing God how much we love him. So, the next time you open up a brand new box of crayons, think of how boring it would be if you only had red to color with. Let it remind you of how much God values differences in people and how He wants us to treat others that are different from us.

Let's Talk About the Story

What is your favorite color?
Do you think God has a favorite color?
What does "equal" mean?
Who does God bless when they follow Him?

The next time you see someone different from you, think about the rainbow and how dull it would be if it didn't have so many lovely colors. Remember how God wants you to treat those people that are different from you and thank God for the differences.

Prayer

Dear God,

Thank you for all the beautiful colors in your world. Thank you for different people, too. Help me to treat people that are different from me the way I want to be treated. Thank you for loving us and creating us equal. I love you God. Amen

Family Activities

Talk about differences in people. Come up with ways that your children can treat others that are different from them. Help your children discover ways that children are more alike than they are different. Pray for those children who are disadvantaged, and pray that your child may develop a tender heart to those that are in some way different.

References: Genesis 11:1–9; Proverbs 27:2; Matthew 7:1,12; Matthew 22:39; Philippians 2:3; James 2:1

February—A Basketful of Fruit

Ding-dong, the door bell rang again. Mrs. Miller slowly walked to the front door to see who was there—not really wanting to visit with anyone on this particular day. As she opened the door, she saw a man standing at on the porch holding a bouquet of beautiful flowers and a basket of fruit. "These are for Shannon Miller. Is she home?"

"Why, yes, I'm Shannon Miller," she said as she graciously reached for the bundle in his arms. *Who could these possibly be from* she wondered to herself as she thanked the gentleman and said goodbye. Once inside, Shannon sat the flowers and fruit on the table and looked for a note to tell her who had sent them. As she read the note that was attached to the flowers, tears streamed down her cheeks. It said, "Love, from Julie and Jeffrey." Such a simple phrase, yet it meant so much to Shannon.

Today was Valentine's Day. Since Mrs. Miller's husband had passed away a few months ago, this was the first Valentine's Day to have spent alone after 60 years of marriage. She didn't feel like smiling or being happy. Edward, her husband, had always made occasions like today very special for her, always remembering the little things that made her smile. But today was different. She could only think of her best friend and husband, who was no longer with her. But now, the flowers and the fruit, they did warm her heart, even though she was reluctant to admit it. Julie and Jeffrey were two of the neighborhood children who lived across the street. Mrs. Miller had known them since they were babies. Jeffrey used to come over and play catch with Mr. Miller after school when his dad was still at work, and Julie would come over and visit with Mrs. Miller and help in the flower bed. They were sad too when their friend and neighbor, Mr. Miller passed away suddenly. The memories of watching the two small children playing in the yard and visiting with them brought a quick smile to her face. The children were almost grown now at 16 and 18 years of age, but they still came to visit when they could. But to send flowers and fruit on a day like today seemed extra-ordinary to Mrs. Miller. She sat down to smell the flowers. They were the same kind her husband used to send to her every year. Quiet tears again rolled across her cheeks at pleasant memories of the many years gone by. Though she could understand the flowers being sent, she still couldn't figure out why they had sent the fruit. Mr. Miller never gave her fruit as a gift—only tulips or roses.

She turned the basket of oranges, pears, and apples around to look at the other side. *What nice pieces of fruit were gathered in the basket* she thought to herself. Then almost by surprise, she noticed a slip of paper slid in the corner of the basket. She took it out to see what it was and found this note:

"Dear Mrs. Miller, Jeffrey and I wanted to let you know that we are thinking of you today. We hope you enjoy the fruit. We are sending it to you because we always think of you when we eat a piece of fruit. We still remember the day you taught us about the Fruit of the Spirit. You told us that in the book of Galatians, Paul lists all the Fruits of the Spirit that should easily be seen in our lives if we are living the kind of life that would please God. Then, you took us out to show us the fruit tree in your backyard. You pointed to an orange tree and asked us what kind of tree it was and how we knew. You also asked us how confused we would feel if the orange tree sometimes grew apples instead of oranges. We laughed at that question, but you were right. If an orange tree grew apples, no one would know what kind of tree it was supposed to be or what kind of fruit to expect from it. People would not trust those trees and would be confused. You said that's how it is in our lives as well. If we say we are Christians but don't act like it, people can't trust us. They won't know we are Christians. Then God can't use us the way He wants to . . . just like we couldn't use the orange tree the way we

would want if it sometimes grew apples. We couldn't have fresh squeezed orange juice for breakfast each morning if we never knew if it was going to have apples or oranges on it. We want God to use us the way we were meant to be used by Him. Thank you for teaching us an important lesson on a day when all we could do was argue and fight. We love you and hope you have a happy Valentine's Day.

Love, Jeffrey and Julie

After Mrs. Miller finished reading the letter, she wiped the tears from her eyes and smiled her biggest smile since her husband died. Today was Valentine's Day. Maybe Edward wouldn't be sending her flowers, but she got something even better . . . a basketful of fruit.

Let's Think About the Fruit of the Spirit

What is your favorite kind of fruit?

Have you ever seen a fruit tree or a basket of fruit?

What are some ways that your life can be like fruit, letting other people know that you know Jesus?

As you read more about the Fruit of the Spirit this month, think about ways that you can live your life so that others know you love Jesus.

Week One–Fruit of the Spirit

Galatians 5:22–23
But the fruit of the spirit is love, joy, peace, patience, kindness, goodness, faithfulness, gentleness and self-control. Against such things there is no law. (NIV)

But the fruit of the Spirit is love, joy, peace, longsuffering, gentleness, goodness, faith, meekness, temperance: against such there is no law. (KJV)

Jeffrey and Julie were once again fighting. This time it

was over the television remote, last time it was over who got to sit where in the living room. Who knows what it would be about next time. They seem to fight all the time over little things that really don't make a difference one way or the other. One day as they were fighting, their neighbor Gregory was over. Gregory's family didn't go to church like Jeffrey and Julie's family did. They went every Sunday and even on Wednesdays too. Jeffrey and Julie didn't see the point in so much church. But they didn't have a choice; they had to go. Their dad even led family devotions where he read the Bible to them and talked about what the verses meant; then they prayed together as a family. Their family was Christian and they heard about Christ all the time it seemed. Gregory's family, on the other hand, never went to church. He didn't even much know who Jesus was except that he heard something about a baby Jesus at Christmas time.

All three kids were about the same age. Jeffrey and Julie were 12 and 14, while Gregory was 13. They hadn't been friends long since Gregory's family had only recently moved to the neighborhood, but they all liked each other and got along well. As they were fighting again over who got to sit where in the family room, Gregory had finally had enough. "Why are y'all fighting again?" he asked. "You fight all the time."

Julie and Jeffrey looked at each other and together said, "No we don't."

Gregory wasn't going to let them off that easily so he said, "You know, y'all sound just like my parents. They fight all the time. I get sick of hearing people yelling at each other and calling people names. I thought it would be different over here because you go to church and talk about doing things with your family, but it's no different with you two than it is with my mom and dad. I don't get it."

With that, Julie and Jeffrey suddenly got quiet. Did they really fight that much? Was it so obvious to everyone but them? Both apologized to Gregory as he was heading out the door. But did it do any good? Would their behavior change, or would

Gregory even believe them and want to still play with them? Neither Jeffrey nor Julie felt like playing after that, so each went to their own rooms to be alone and think. A few hours later when they were not quite so angry at each other, they began to talk about what Gregory had said.

"What Gregory said made me mad," said Jeffrey. "He acts like he knows everything."

"I think what he said made sense," Julie said. "Why would he make up something like that if it weren't true?"

"No way! You think we act as bad as his parents do, too!" exclaimed Jeffrey.

I don't know if we act as bad as they do, but I know we don't act like mom and dad have taught us to act. We do fight a lot and call each other names. It made me feel bad when he said that we aren't any different than his own family. We should be different, Jeffrey. We go to church and we have parents that have taught us how to be kind and patient, how to use self-control even when we're mad, and how to love each other. I don't think we are doing that very well if Gregory can't even tell the difference in our lives. Mom and Dad sure don't fight like we do. They say they love each other and they act like it."

"Maybe you're right. It's hard to always be nice though. I don't want to always share and be kind and loving. Sometimes I just want my own way," Jeffrey said with a little bit of sadness in his voice.

"I know what you mean. I feel the same way", commented Julie. "Remember what Mrs. Miller taught us about the Fruit of the Spirit? And then last week our Sunday School lesson was on it too. The Fruit of the Spirit is love, joy, peace, patience, kindness, goodness, faithfulness, gentleness, and self-control."

Jeffrey responded, "Yeah, I remember all those; it's just hard to keep doing them. But I think I need to start working on them a little more, even if it means I won't always get my way. I remember learning that God will help us when things are hard if we ask Him. I think I need to ask Him right now."

"Let's both ask Him for help to be more kind, patient, and loving towards each other, starting today."

Let's Talk About the Story

What were Julie and Jeffrey fighting over?

Who heard them fight?

What did Gregory say about their constant fighting? Did he like it?

Do you ever argue with someone like a brother or sister? Do you think you could find a better way to talk to that person rather than fighting and arguing?

What are three of the Fruit of the Spirit that Julie talked about?

Why is it important that others be able to see fruit in our own lives?

This week as you play with friends or your family members, remember how important it is that the Fruit of the Spirit be very obvious in your words, your play, and your thoughts. Ask God to help you if you feel an argument about to start.

Prayer

Dear Father,

Thank you for teaching us about the Fruit of the Spirit and how important it is in our lives. Help me to show your fruit everyday so that others will know that I love you and that I'm a Christian. Amen.

Family Activity

Sometime during the week take time to look at various kinds of fruit or at a few fruit trees if they grow where you live. Discuss the differences in kinds of fruit and what each person's favorite fruit is. Then talk about why it's important that our lives demonstrate the fruit of God's spirit each and every day. Without His fruit being evident in our lives, we'd be like an apple tree that never grew apples. No one would know what kind of tree we were if we didn't have the fruit on it to prove what we were. Make some homemade food from fruit such as apple pie, apple sauce, peach preserves, or banana bread and thank God for the fruit He gives us and especially for the Fruit of the Spirit.

References: Matthew 7:20, John 15:16, Colossians 3: 12-14

Week Two—What is Love

1 Corinthians 13:13
And now these three remain: faith, hope and love. But the greatest of these is love. (NIV)

And now abideth faith, hope, charity, these three; but the greatest of these is charity. (KJV)

"Trenton, would you like to have pizza for supper tonight?" Mom asked 5 year old Trenton one snowy evening.

"I *love* pizza! Of course I want it for supper!" he exclaimed in a loud voice.

Later that evening after the family had eaten their pizza, Mom brought out brownies that had been cooling in the kitchen. "Anyone care for some warm brownies?"

"I do, I do," shouted Trenton from the living room where he and his dad were building a fort. "I *love* brownies. They're my favorite!" Mom served them both some warm brownies with milk then sat down to read a book while they finished their fort.

"Look at our cool fort, Mom. This is the best fort we've ever built. I *love* building forts with Daddy. He's fun to play with."

Mom complimented her son on the fort and then told him it was time to get ready for bed. "I'll read *Goodnight Moon* to you two times after you've brushed your teeth."

"Oh, goody, I *love Goodnight Moon,* it's my favorite story," Trenton cried out in a very happy voice.

After his teeth were brushed and the story had been read twice, Mom tucked him into bed. "Good night Trenton, I love you."

"Good night, Mom. I *love* you too."

Just then Mom had an idea. "Trenton do you love me more than pizza?"

Giggling, Trenton said, "Of course I do."

"Do you love me more than warm brownies and milk?" she asked.

"Yep, even more than those, but I do like them a lot." he said with a smile.

"How about more than *Goodnight Moon*—twice. Do you love me more than that?"

With a smile, Trenton reached up and hugged his mom tight and told her that he loved her even more than his very favorite story.

"Well honey, tonight you told me that you loved each one of those things, and then you said that you loved me too. How do I know that you love me more than those other things?"

"I don't know. How?"

Mom thought a moment and then said, "Sometimes we use the word 'love' too much and then when we really feel love for someone, it sounds confusing. Our love should be reserved only for God and for people like moms, dads, grandparents or even pets, like your fish Ziggy. It's not wrong to say that you love pizza and brownies, but always make sure that you know the difference. Real love, from the heart, shouldn't be wasted on things like forts, books, and food. Let's save our real love for God and for the people He has given us."

"Okay, Mom, good night. I *LOVE* you." This time Trenton said it with a twinkle in his eyes and a big bear hug to go along with it. Mom knew he meant it.

"Goodnight, Son. I *love* you too, very much." Then she tiptoed to the door and turned out the light.

Let's Talk About the Story

Name three things that Trenton said he loved?

What did Mom say about real love that comes from the heart?

What does the Bible say is the most important: faith, hope, or love?

This week as you eat yummy foods, watch a favorite movie, or play a favorite game, see how many times you use the word 'love.' Do you really love that game as much as you love your mom and dad? Make sure that the people you love know that you love them more than anything else.

Prayer

Dear Father,

Thank you so much for loving us. Thank you for teaching us about love and for giving us so many things to enjoy. Help us this week to show our real love to those that we love and to remember how important it is to tell our family that we love them every day. I love you God. Amen

Family Activity

Have a game night where you play each person's favorite game. Have them tell what it is that they like about the game before they play and then ask if they still like it when the game is over, even if they lost. Finally, before going to bed, have each person tell other family members that they love them and why.

References: Matthew 5:44, John 13: 34–35; 1 Corinthians 13:8, 1 Corinthians 13:4, 1 Peter 4:8

Week Three—Kindest Attitude

Ephesians 4:32
Be kind and compassionate to one another, * forgiving each other, just as in Christ God forgave you. (NIV)

And be ye kind one to another, * tenderhearted, forgiving one another, even as God for Christ's sake hath forgiven you. (KJV)

Autumn walked in the kitchen holding a certificate of honor in her hand. She handed it to her mom who read it then gave her daughter a big, happy hug. The award was presented to Autumn at school for having the kindest attitude in the class. Her mother was very proud of her daughter, and she would have to agree, Autumn usually did demonstrate a very kind attitude towards everyone. Autumn didn't look as happy though. She didn't seem to care about the award. "What's wrong, Autumn? Aren't you happy with this special award?" Mother asked. Autumn didn't answer; she just stared out the window. A few minutes later, her mother brought her some hot chocolate with marshmallows on top, one of Autumn's favorite drinks. As she drank the warm cocoa, dodging the marshmallows as she slowly sipped, she began to tell her mom about the other kids in class.

"Mom, Sarah got an award too. She got the best artist award. And Dillon got the best sportsman award. Oh, and Michelle got the best helper award."

"Those are all impressive awards, honey, but I don't think they are any more impressive than yours."

"I do. What's so special about 'kindest attitude' anyway? I don't even know what it means."

"Honey, do you remember what the Bible tells us about being kind to others? It says that we are to be kind to everyone, which means to be nice to them. We are to forgive and be understanding towards people who are hurting, who are in trouble, or even towards those that don't treat us very nice. If we do that we are showing God's love to the world. Having the 'kindest attitude' in the class means that you are showing God's love to everyone in your class without even knowing you are doing it. That's why I am so proud of you. Without kindness, people wouldn't have friends. And no one wants to go to a doctor or have a teacher that is impatient or rude, or mean. We all want to be around people who have a kind attitude. Does that make more sense now?"

"Yes, I guess so. 'Kindest attitude' sounds better now. Maybe I should go hang the award up in my room where I can see it every day, and it can remind me to always be kind to everyone."

"I think that would be a wonderful idea. Why don't we go do it right now?"

Let's Talk About the Story

What kind of award did Autum receive at school?

How did she feel about it? How did her mom feel about the award?

What does having a kind attitude mean?

Can you think of someone who is easy to be kind to? Someone who is hard to be kind to? Are you always easy for others to be kind to?

As you work on the memory verse this week, think about ways that you can show kindness to others, especially those that might not be very nice to you.

Prayer

Dear Father,

Thank you for being kind and patient with us, even when we aren't very kind to others. Help us to have a kinder attitude at home and at school even when we don't feel like it. Amen

Family Activity

Try doing something different as a family this week that would show compassion to others. You might visit a nursing home, bake a pie or cookies for a neighbor, or help someone who is having a hard time. As you involve the family in the activity, remind your children of the scripture verse and how your actions are displaying Christ's love to others.

References Verses: Matthew 7: 12; John 15: 17; Galatians 6:10; 1 Thessalonians 5:15

Week Four—Self Controlled, not Remote Controlled

1 Peter 5:8–9a
Be self-controlled and alert.* Your enemy the devil prowls around like a roaring lion looking for someone to devour. Resist him, standing firm in the faith. (NIV)

Be sober, be vigilant;* because your adversary the devil, as a roaring lion, walketh about, seeking whom he may devour; whom resist steadfast in the faith . . . (KJV)

Ryan was angry. His sister had taken the last of the cookies and he didn't think it was fair. Even though he had just returned from a friend's house, and she didn't know he wanted any cookies, he was so mad he pushed her then tore the paper she had just finished coloring for her teacher. Ryan's dad saw what happened and sent Ryan to his room for time-out, or time to think about his actions.

After being in his room for what seemed a very long time to seven-year-old Ryan, his dad appeared beside his bed. It was obvious that Ryan had been crying. His dad was sorry that his son was hurting but was relieved to see that he was feeling bad for his actions. "Ryan, I think we need to talk."

"I don't want to talk to you," Ryan said with his head still in the pillow.

"Okay, then you listen, and I'll talk," Dad said in a very fatherly tone. "Ryan, what you did to your sister was not very nice. She didn't do anything to deserve that kind of treatment from you. You reacted to something that made you mad before you took the time to think it through."

Ryan raised his head up from the pillow and sniffed as he dried the tears from his eyes. "But I wanted those cookies. They were my favorite kind and now we're out. It's not fair!"

"You may not see it as fair, but that doesn't give you the right to hurt people or to destroy their belongings. Your temper took control of you rather than you having control of it. Think of it as being similar to your remote control car that runs by someone else controlling it. When we lose our temper it is as if someone else or something else is in control of us rather than ourselves. Being in control of yourself is known as 'self-control' and it is one of the fruits of the Spirit that we read about in the Bible. Having self-control means being in control of your emotions and your actions, even when you are angry. Without learning to use good self-control, you will end up hurting others and hurting yourself as well. Remember when the person handling the controls on your car gets silly or lazy, the car wrecks and doesn't go in the direction it should be going, right? That's how it is with our own lives when we don't keep control of our emotions. The devil, or Satan, wants us to loose our temper. He's always looking and waiting for someone to get mad and make a mistake with what they say or in what they do. You're hurting yourself when you act in anger, before you think."

"How does it hurt myself," asked Ryan?

"By cheating yourself out of fun and by disappointing yourself are just two ways you can hurt yourself by not using self-control," Dad explained.

"I get it. I'm sorry for getting mad at Sarah and for ruining her picture. I guess I need better self-control, huh Dad?"

Dad answered, "Well, yes, that would sure help you in your relationships with others. I bet if you apologize to Sarah and ask her forgiveness, she'd forgive you. You can't fix her picture, but maybe you can help make it up to her by spending some time coloring with her."

Let's Talk About the Story

What did Sarah do that made Ryan so angry?
Did Ryan react in a proper way?
What would have been a better way for Ryan to handle his anger?
What does the Bible tell us about self-control?

Prayer

Dear Father,
Thank you for being patient with us and not getting angry like we do when we mess up. Help us to use better self-control when things don't go our way. Help us to be more patient and understanding of others too. Amen.

Family Activity

Use opportunities this week to explore self-control. Compliment each other when self-control is observed. Such times might include turning the TV off when doing homework, eating only two cookies instead of five, choosing to go to bed earlier on a night before a big test or game, as well as controlling tempers when something makes somebody angry. Refer to the memory verse as a reminder of how God wants us to respond in times of temptation.

References: Psalm 29: 11; 1 Peter 1:13; 1 Peter 4:7

Luke and John were excited that Easter was almost here. Their parents had decorated the house with cute little bunnies, yellow fuzzy chicks, and brightly colored eggs. They talked about all the candy they would get from the Easter Bunny and how fun it would be to have another Easter egg hunt. Both boys couldn't wait until Sunday morning. It was just two days away.

Mom had already taken the four-year-old twins out shopping for new Easter clothes to wear to church on Sunday. They had new Sunday shoes, new pants, suspenders to match, and a new shirt. Fancy clothes weren't their favorite, they'd much rather be in jeans and sneakers, but they could handle the clothes and pictures that Mom would surely make if it meant candy, eggs, and lots of surprises. Mom was even preparing a big Sunday lunch with ham, rolls and lots of other yummy food. Grandma and Grandpa were coming over for the Sunday meal. The Easter Bunny must be special, the twins decided, if Mom is going to all of this trouble.

On Saturday, Mom, Dad, and the boys colored eggs. They had a great time choosing different colors to dye their eggs and seeing whose was the prettiest, the most creative, and the most unique. No one even cracked an egg. After they were through and the kitchen was cleaned up, Daddy sat down on the floor to read Luke and John their bedtime story. They were hoping for "The Little Engine that Could," but Daddy had a new book in his hands. He also had his Bible out.

"Hey boys, come sit down by me and let's read a new book." Luke and John did as Daddy said. Mother sat next to them. "Tonight I want to read a new story to you. This is the story about Easter."

"Yeah! We like hearing about the Easter Bunny, he's cool."

"I don't think that's what this story is about," said Mother. "Why don't you listen to Daddy and see what he's going to read to you."

"Mommy's right. This story isn't about the Easter Bunny. This is the story about the real meaning of Easter. This is the story of Jesus."

"We know about Jesus. You've told us about Him before, and we heard about Him in church too," the boys said together. "He was born in a manger."

"Well, yes, Jesus was born in a manger. That's why we celebrate Christmas. But Easter is about a different part of Jesus' life. Easter is about something special Jesus did as a man. Something He did for all of us, many, many years ago."

As Daddy read the Easter story to Luke and John they listened intently. Afterward, he asked them questions about the story. When the story ended, Luke had a sad look on his face. Mom asked him what was wrong. "It's just that Jesus was nice to everyone. Why did they have to be mean back to him? That's not fair. I don't like that part of the story."

"You're right, Luke," Daddy began. "It doesn't sound fair and it was a very mean thing to do, but that's the way it had to be. God loved us all so much that He needed Jesus to die on the cross for our sins so that we could live in heaven with Him. Without Jesus being willing to obey God and die for our sins, we wouldn't know God today. Jesus made the way for us to get to God, even though we don't deserve it. Now that doesn't sound so mean does it?"

"No way," John interrupted as he rolled around on the floor. "Jesus did a good thing when He died on the cross, but He did a super-duper thing when He was 'resected' from the dead."

"Do you mean, 'resurrected,' John?" Daddy asked.

"Yeah, r-e-surr-ec-ted. Is that what Easter is about, Daddy, Jesus dying on the cross?"

"That's right, Jesus dying for our sins, and then being brought back to life again on the third day. That's called the res-urrection. That's what Easter is all about, new life."

"We may buy you new clothes, new shoes and have Eas-ter egg hunts, but that's just for fun. It's not really what Easter means to Christians," Mom said as she held John in her lap. "And so we celebrate Easter with new things to remember the new life that we can have in Jesus."

With that, both boys had settled down, John now with his head on Mom's shoulder and Luke was in Daddy's lap. Daddy led them in prayer before carrying them to bed for the night. They needed to get a good night's sleep. Tomorrow promised to be a busy day. They were going to celebrate the resurrection of Jesus.

Let's Think About Easter

What were Luke and John looking forward to at the beginning of the story?

Who was coming for lunch on Sunday?

What did Daddy say the real meaning of Easter was?

As you learn more about the real meaning of Easter this month, take time to thank God for new life in Him. Thank Him for loving us so much that He wanted to share heaven with us.

Week One–What is Sin?

Romans 5:8
But God demonstrates his own love for us in this: While we were still sinners, Christ died for us. (NIV)

But God commendeth his love toward us, in that, while we were yet sinners, Christ died for us. (KJV)

"Kayla, time for your bath," Mother called to her eight-year-old daughter who was busy playing outside.

"I don't want to take a bath right now. Do I have to?" asked Kayla.

"Yes, come in right now. Picture day is tomorrow, and you need be clean so you can look your best at school."

Soon, Kayla came in and Mother helped her start her bath and wash her hair. Afterward, Kayla had time to play with her toys in the warm water before she dried off and put on her princess gown with matching pink slippers. Mother was preparing to dry her hair when Kayla asked, "Mom, where does all the dirt go after my bath?"

"That's a very good question, Kayla. Tell me where you think the dirt goes."

"I don't know, but I think it goes down into a little dirt catcher at the bottom of the drain, then it gets put back out in the yard so we can play in it again the next day and we never run out of dirt. That's what I think."

"What an interesting thought. I like that idea," Mom said. "Actually the dirt becomes part of the water and washes down the drain with it. It isn't separated from the water so it can't be put back into the yard for another day of fun. But I like your idea. You know Kayla, your question reminds me of something the Bible teaches us."

"It does? What? Does the Bible talk about taking baths too?"

"Not exactly, but what it does talk about is sin. Do you remember what sin is?"

"Kinda, but it's hard to explain I think. Can you tell me what sin is Mom?"

"Sure, Honey. Sin is anything we do that goes against what God says to do. Sin hurts God because He knows it isn't what is best for us and it breaks His heart. Sin is like the dirt from the bath water. Our lives are filled with sin. We can't get rid of it though like we can dirt from the backyard. We can't just wash it away with soap and water. Sin makes us dirty on the inside. So dirty in fact that the Bible says God can't even look at our hearts. It's not real dirt, but we are still considered unclean to God. But because God loves us so much, He wanted to scrub us clean from the inside out. That's why He sent Jesus to die on the cross for our sins. Jesus is like the water that cleanses us on the outside, but Jesus cleanses us on the inside. He gets rid of our sin so that God can look at our hearts and see only clean . . . a pure white kind of clean."

"Mom, does everybody have sin in their hearts, or just the bad people that are in jail?"

"The Bible tells us that everybody is a sinner. We all sin and need to be forgiven or cleansed. And just like the bath water, once Jesus cleanses us on the inside, our sin is washed away like the dirt in the bathwater. We will never see the dirt again and God will never see the sin again. We will still do wrong things and hurt God, but because of Jesus, God will always see us as white as this brand new towel."

"Wow! That's really white," Kayla exclaimed. "God must love us a lot to make us that clean even when we do things that hurt His feelings."

"Yes, He sure does, and so do I. Now, let's finish drying your hair so you can go to bed. You have a big day tomorrow, and I know you want to look your best for your pictures."

Let's Talk About the Story

Where had Kayla been when her mom called her inside?

What do you think she had been playing?

Do you like to play in the dirt?

What did her mom say that sin was like?

Can you explain what sin is?

Prayer

Dear Father,

Thank you for soap, warm baths and clean towels. Thank you for making dirt so much fun too. Forgive us for sinning against you and hurting you. Help us to follow you more closely so that our sin doesn't keep us from you. Amen.

Family Activity

After a good rain, go outside and make mud pies. Squish your feet and hands in the mud and talk about how different dirt and mud makes us look. After washing in the water hose, remind the kids that washing up after playing in the mud is similar to what Jesus does for us when He comes into our heart and cleanses us from our sins. Then, thank Him for His forgiveness. Also, read over the words together to the hymns, "Are You Washed in the Blood of the Lamb" and "Nothing but the Blood."

References: Isaiah 59:2; Romans 3: 23; Romans 6: 23; James 4:17

Week Two—Mercy Me!

Ephesians 2:8–9
For it is by grace you have been saved, through faith*—and this not from yourselves, it is the gift of God—not by works, so that no one can boast. (NIV)

For by grace are ye saved through faith;* and that not of yourselves; it is the gift of God; not of works, lest any man should boast. (KJV)

"Okay, okay . . . ," cried Jeremy. "Mercy, Mercy, I give up!" Jeremy and his big brother Zac were playing the hand wrestling game called "Mercy!" where the first person to call out mercy loses while the other is deemed the winner. Zac liked to play the game with his younger brother. It made him feel strong and powerful, and he never really hurt Jeremy anyway, it was all in fun.

Grandpa came in to check on the boys. From all the raucous sounds, he wasn't sure if someone was hurt or not. "Hey fella's," called Grandpa from the hallway. "What's going on in there? You two sound like your having a real knock down, drag out fight. Are you alright?"

"Oh, hi Grandpa," the boys said in unison. "We're fine. We're just playing the game 'Mercy.'"

"And I won!" yelled out Zac. "I made Jeremy cry out Mercy first, so I win."

"I remember that game. Isn't that where you try to hurt your partner by bending his fingers back until he shouts?" Grandpa inquired quietly.

"Yes sir. It may sound mean, but it's really fun." Both boys looked like they were having a good time, although Grandpa didn't think he would enjoy it anymore at his age.

"That's an ironic name for a game of pain. Have you ever stopped to think about the meaning of the word mercy?

"No not really. Grandpa, is this going to be another story about how you had to walk miles to school every day so we should be thankful for school buses?"

"No boys, it's not. I just thought it would be fun to see what the word mercy really means. Mercy is a word used in the Bible to describe God's love toward us. God had mercy on us when He saw that we were full of sin, and yet He chose to die for us. His mercy is what saves us."

"That sounds like our game, Grandpa. When Jeremy calls out and I know he means it, I stop. I save him from the pain he might feel if I kept going."

"That's right, Zac. When God gives us good things that we haven't earned, that's GRACE. And when he holds something yucky back from us that we have earned, but in His love He chooses not to give it to us, that's called MERCY. If one of you boys broke your grandmother's vase because you were playing ball in the house, she would be very upset. You would deserve to be punished because you know what the rules are in the house. But if she chose to, she could change her mind and have mercy on you. You deserve punishment, but she could offer you an understanding hug instead. Sometimes when people do nice things to us, it makes us feel worse than punishment does, and it makes us think. Many times that's what God does with us. He offers us something like a hug instead of punishment, and He forgives us over and over again. That's what mercy is all about. When we call out to Him with a sincere heart, like you do in your game, He hears us and offers us His Mercy. Even though He is more powerful than we are and has the authority to do anything, He chooses to show mercy so that we might show mercy to others."

"Wow, Grandpa," Jeremy said. "That sure makes our game take on a different meaning. It doesn't make it sound as much fun anymore. But I like the mercy and grace thing God does for us. That is way better than any game we could play."

Let's Talk About the Story

What were Zac and Jeremy playing?

Who won?

What does the Bible tell us the real meaning of Mercy is?

What is Grace?

Prayer

Dear Father,

Thank you for teaching us about Grace and Mercy. You sure must love us a lot to do so much for us. Help us to show Grace and Mercy to others too when they don't deserve it, just like you do to us when we least deserve it. Amen.

Family Activity

Take time out to explain various ways that grace and mercy have been used in practical ways throughout the week. If punishment was in order but you chose to sit down and talk and end it with a hug, that's mercy. If the kids had been arguing but you knew it had been a long day inside with bad weather so you chose to trade punishment for a trip to the movie instead, that's grace. For an easy way to remember the difference between grace and mercy, explain that *grace* begins with the letter *G* as does *give,* while mercy doesn't, so it's about withholding, not giving.

References: Romans 8: 34–35; Titus 2:11; 1 Peter 1: 3–4

Week Three–Forgive Me, Forgive Me Not

I John 1:9
If we confess our sins, he is faithful and will forgive us our sins* and purify us from all unrighteousness. (NIV)

If we confess our sins, he is faithful and just to forgive us our sins,* and to cleanse us from all unrighteousness. (KJV)

Six-year-old Lauren ran in the house in tears. Her best friend Rachel hurt her feelings and she was angry. It was the third time this week. She was never going to play with her again. Not ever! Lauren sat on her bright pink bean bag chair in the corner of her bedroom and began to remember everything that Rachel had done to her that was mean. The best she could figure she was up to 16 things and still counting.

Knock, knock, knock. "Lauren, may I come in." It was her Aunt Beth. Lauren loved Aunt Beth. She always made her feel better whenever she was sad about something.

"I guess so," said a sad Lauren. The door quietly opened

and Aunt Beth walked in, finding a soft spot on the rug next to Lauren's oversized chair where she still sat.

"I heard you and Rachel got in another argument today. Want to talk about it."

"Rachel always makes me mad. She doesn't play fair, so I'm never going to be her friend again."

"That sounds serious. She must have done something really mean for you to feel this way."

"Yes she did."

"Tell me why you were her friend in the first place." With that, Lauren began, thinking of all the funny things Rachel did and how much fun the two girls had when together. Lauren was already smiling and laughing before her aunt stopped her.

"Lauren it seems like Rachel is a pretty good friend. Sounds like you've had some great times together. I sure would hate to lose a friend like that. Wouldn't you?"

"Maybe," answered Lauren, not sure what her aunt was going to say next.

"Lauren, I know that Rachel may have hurt your feelings very badly. That never feels good. I don't like it when my feelings get hurt either. I know how that feels. But, when someone is as good a friend as Rachel seems to be, maybe forgiving her is the better thing to do, rather than staying mad at her."

"But why Aunt Beth? She must not like me very much if she keeps making me mad all the time. Why should I forgive her?"

"Well, have you ever done anything that made her mad at you?"

Lauren shamefully nodded her head and kept her eyes down.

"Jesus tells us that we need to forgive others like He forgives us. When Jesus died on the cross for us, He offered us forgiveness. Nobody has ever hurt anyone as much as we hurt Jesus when He died on the cross for our sins. If He can forgive us, I bet we can learn how to forgive our friends too. Forgiveness can be hard to do, but it's the best way to keep a best friend. Besides, I don't think Rachel really meant to hurt you. Maybe you hurt her by something you said in your anger too. Why don't we go to her house and see if she'd like to walk to the park and play for a while. We could talk it out and maybe even share a laugh or two."

"Alright Aunt Beth, but first, let me get my jacket. It may get cold before we come home."

Let's Talk About the Story

What were the names of the two friends in the story?
Why did Lauren come home in tears?
What did Jesus do for us on the cross?
Tell about a time when you got angry at someone.
Have you ever made someone mad at you? How did you make it right?

Prayer

Dear Father,
Thank you for forgiving us for our sins. Help us to forgive others even when we don't want to. Thank you for your salvation too that comes through forgiveness. Amen.

Family Activity

Plan a time when you can visit a nursing home or an older couple still married from your neighborhood or church. Talk to them about how their marriage has lasted so long and if forgiveness played a role in their long relationship. Send them a homemade card later to thank them for their time and words of wisdom.

References: Psalm 103: 12; John 3:16; I Timothy 1:15; I Timothy 2:4–5; I John 4:10–11

Week Four—New Life on the Farm

II Corinthians 5:17
Therefore, if anyone is in Christ, he is a new creation; the old has gone, the new has come! (NIV)

Therefore if any man be in Christ, he is a new creature; old things are passed away; behold, all things are become new. (KJV)

Hope and Grace couldn't wait to get started on their chores. Their pig Petunia was due to have babies any moment, and they didn't want to miss the exciting event. They knew their chores would have to be done before they could take time out to see the new piglets so they hurriedly worked around the house, cleaning their rooms, gathering eggs, and washing dishes.

Soon the time had come for Petunia to give birth. Chores were finished just in time, so the two sisters ran out to the pig pen where Petunia lay in the hay. Five pink little piglets had already been born but more were due. Within the hour five more squeaky little pigs lay next to their mother, searching for milk to fill their empty tummies. The girls eagerly welcomed ten noisy little babies as Petunia proudly slept nearby. New life had come to the farm today and the girls were thrilled. They wanted to tell their friends as soon as possible, but their Dad had a different idea.

"Girls," he said, as if they were in trouble. Bring me a Bible and come back out here to the pen. "I'd like to read something to you."

Hope knew where her Daddy's Bible was so she ran to get it and within moments was back, sitting atop a small pile of hay.

Their Dad began, "Today when I experienced the miracle of life happen with Petunia, I couldn't help but think of all the new life going on around us on the farm every day. The trees are turning green. The tulips and roses are budding, and the grass is green again. Bluebonnets are all around the hillside. All these are signs of new life after a long, silent winter."

"Dad, I saw the robin's nest yesterday when you were gone. The eggs have already hatched now!"

"I saw a neighbor's cat, Frosty, with her four kittens too. They were born last week," Hope said with excitement.

"That's right. All these things are signs of life. But do you know what's even more exciting than kittens and piglets? It's having new life in Christ. When we accept Jesus as the only way of salvation and turn to Him as our Savior, He gives us new life on the inside. Jesus died on the cross and was resurrected on the third day in order for us to experience that brand new life. We may get excited about having pretty new dresses, shoes and hats for church on Easter Sunday, but having new life in Christ is far more exciting."

"Dad, since tomorrow is Easter, can we bring pictures of Petunia's piglets to church to help explain to our friends what new life is really all about?" Grace asked enthusiastically.

"I think that would be a good idea, Grace. Now, let's find the camera and I'll take some pictures."

Let's Talk About the Story

Name some things that come to life in the spring?

What are some things that Hope and Grace mentioned in the story that had recently been given life?

What does Jesus' resurrection mean to us?

Can you tell what Easter and the resurrection is really about?

Prayer

Dear Father,

Thank you for new life. Thank you for springtime and all the beautiful flowers that are blooming and the bright colors all around us. Mostly, though, thank you for giving us new life through your son Jesus, who was resurrected from the dead on the third day. Amen.

References: Isaiah 65:17; Matthew 28:5–7; Mark 16:6; John 20: 21; 1 Corinthians 15:52; 1 Thessalonians 4:13–18; 1 Peter 1: 23; Revelation 3: 20

April—What is a Christian?

Thomas and David were friends. In fact, they were more than friends, they were best friends. They had known each other for a long time, but Thomas had never spent the night at David's house. This weekend was different because Thomas's parents had to go out of town, so he was allowed to spend two nights with his best friend. The boys were so excited and had been talking about their plans all week at school.

When Thomas finally arrived at David's house, the boys played baseball, basketball, video games, and watched a movie. They even jumped on the trampoline. After a full day of playing on Saturday, David's mother told the boys it was time to get ready for bed. They didn't like hearing that because it meant an end to their day of fun. They knew better than to disobey however, so they promptly followed instructions and dressed for bed. Thomas knew that they had to go to bed earlier than usual because David's family went to church on Sunday mornings. They would need to get up earlier tomorrow morning to make it on time. Thomas' family never went to church so he was excited about seeing what church was all about, but he was a bit scared too. Soon he drifted off to sleep and didn't awake until David's dad woke them bright and early the next morning.

After dressing and eating breakfast, the family left for church. In Sunday School, Thomas saw many new kids plus a few kids he knew from school, but he didn't know they went to church. He had a good time singing the new songs and playing a few Bible games. He heard the teachers talk about being a Christian and reading the Bible. This was all new to him. He had great parents who loved him and his two sisters, but they never talked about the Bible or what being a Christian meant. "Maybe they didn't know either," he thought to himself. After Sunday School,

Thomas went with David and his family to the worship service where they sat together. Again, Thomas heard more about being a Christian and following God, but it still didn't make a lot of sense to him. When the last prayer had been said, everyone filed out of the sanctuary heading to their cars.

Once in the car, David's dad said, "Thomas, you've been awfully quiet this morning. Is everything alright?"

"I'm okay. I just had a lot of questions about what I heard in church today."

"I'd like to try to answer your questions if I could Thomas. What is confusing you the most right now?"

"I want to know what being a Christian is all about. What does that mean?"

"Being a Christian means many different things. It means that you believe that Jesus is the Savior of the world and died on the cross for our sins. It also means that you believe Jesus is the only way to heaven. That's just the beginning though; being a Christian means much more than that. When someone says he is a Christian, his life should look different from those who aren't Christians. He should act differently. The music he listens to should be different, the places he chooses to go and what he chooses to do with his time should all reflect a change on the inside of his heart."

"I knew some of the kids in the Sunday School class today from school, but I never knew they went to church. They don't act any differently. They use bad words that my parents don't even let me use. They even talk about places that they go and movies they've seen that I can't see," Thomas said with some confusion in his voice.

"That is sad when people know the truth and they choose to follow a different path. As Christians we choose to follow Christ so that others will see a difference in our lives. We still get angry and feel sad about things. Life isn't any easier as a Christian than for other people and bad things can still happen to Christians just like everyone else. But we have the Lord to help us when these things occur. We have a relationship with Jesus that helps us through our days. That's what being a Christian means. Our life should be different because we know Christ personally and He has changed us."

Thoughtfully Thomas began to speak again, "May I go with your family to church again next week Mr. Robinson? I always knew that David went to church and I knew he was different from the other guys in class, but I didn't know it was because of God. I thought it was because he had cool parents. Maybe my parents will even want to come with me sometime."

Let's Think About Christianity

What does being a Christian mean?

Should our life look different and be different if we are Christians?

Name some ways that our life should be different to others?

Is being different always bad?

As you study the unit on what being a Christian means this month, think about someone you know who acts like a Christian should act. What makes them seem like a Christian to you?

Week One–Light Your World

Matthew 5:16
In the same way, let your light shine before men,* that they may see your good deeds and praise your Father in heaven.
(NIV)

Let your light so shine before men,* that they may see your good works, and glorify your Father which is in heaven.
(KJV)

Ten-year-old Trey and Preston were going camping with their church mission group for young boys. They both had been camping before with their own families, but never without their parents.

"This should be cool," Preston said as they were loading up the church van. Trey agreed. Twelve other boys from the church, all about their same age, were gathered on the van as well. Everyone was excited as the van took off for the weekend.

When they arrived at the campsite it was nearly supper time. Everyone was hungry but the van needed to be unloaded and the tents set up before anyone could eat. Trey and Preston eagerly got busy setting up camp. The autumn weather was cool and dry. Leaves were floating to the ground, leaving the dry earth covered in a multi- colored blanket. Their leader, Mr. Hernandez was busy gathering wood for the camp fire. Soon it was time for supper. By the time everybody had finished dinner it was dusk. After some time, the leaders called the boys together around the campfire for S'mores and hot chocolate. The warmth of the fire and the hot drinks warmed the boys up quickly. Mr. Hernandez played the guitar and led them in singing. Before sending them for bed however, Mr. Hernandez passed around flashlights for all the boys. As they were being passed around, he began talking to them about the importance of light and all the benefits it brings. The boys chimed in with their thoughts on how beneficial light was to everyday living.

"I know," said Tim, "Light helps us see better."

Charles spoke up too, "Light helps us do our work. Without light we wouldn't be able to work as well."

"Light also helps us find our way if we're lost," said a quiet Philip.

"That's right," replied Mr. Hernandez. "Light does do all those things and we have many different sources from which to get that light. We have candles, electricity, lanterns, and even flashlights like you are holding in your hand. But did you know that you are also a source of light?"

Trey and Preston looked startled at what he said. "How

can we be a light? We aren't lightening bugs, you know." Trey always had something funny to add.

"Boys, the Bible tells us that as Christians we are to be a light to a dark world." With that he began to put out the camp fire. He instructed the boys one at a time to hold up their flash-lights and watch what happens. The ten-year-olds noticed that it got dark very quickly when the fire was put out, but as soon as just one light was held up the area looked much brighter. He motioned for another boy to hold up his light and the campsite got brighter still. As they went around the group, one at a time, each boy held up his flashlight, adding it to the light already glowing. By the time all twelve lights were on, it was amazing how bright the campsite looked. They gasped in amazement.

"That's how it is with our lives. The world is dark because of sin. When Jesus saves us, we become light to a dark world. Jesus wants us to shine our lights so that others will see the way to Him. We can be a light to others by helping them and by being a friend when they may be lonely. By acting like a Christian when no one is around us and by being nice to the person who may not be so nice in return, we are also showing God's light."

With that, Mr. Hernandez led the group in a closing prayer and sent them off to bed. The crickets were chirping. Nearby, Trey and Preston could even hear an owl hooting in the trees. Only the soft embers glowing in the pit was all that was left of the light, but even that was enough to guide the young boys safely to their tent for a cozy night's sleep.

As they walked to their tent, Trey whispered to his best friend, "Wow, I didn't realize how little light it takes to make such a big difference.

Let's Talk About the Story

Where were Trey and Preston going?
What did they do while they were camping?
Who was Mr. Hernandez?
What lesson did he teach them with the flashlights?
How can we be a light to the world?

Prayer

Dear Father,

Thank you for giving us light to help us each day. Help us to be light too so we can show others how to live for you. Amen.

Family Activity

This week schedule some time to play with flashlights in the dark. Explain to the kids how we are to be light in the world just like a flashlight is light to guide us. Turn out the lights and see how dark it is, then add a light and see how much light it provides. Talk about ways that you can be a light in the world.

References: Matthew 5:14; John 14: 15; I Thessalonians 4:7

Week Two–Careful Conduct

James 1:22
Do not merely listen to the word, and so deceive yourselves. Do what it says. (NIV)

But be ye doers of the word, and not hearers only, deceiving your own selves. (KJV)*

Michelle and James were busy playing with their toys when Dad called for them to start their chores. They responded to the request but continued playing. Dad called again for them to come start their chores, and again Michelle and James heard their father's words but chose to ignore what he said. The next time he called, he wasn't as patient. It didn't take long for them to reach their father and ask what he needed done for the day.

Mr. Cox wasn't going to let them off that easily. He had other ideas in mind. "Kids," he began, "Did you hear me when I called you the first time?" Michelle and James both knew better than to lie to their dad so they told the truth.

"Yes, we heard you, Dad."

"Did you understand what I wanted you to do, or were my instructions confusing?"

"No, we knew what you wanted us to do." Both kids looked uncomfortable as they feared they were about to get in trouble for ignoring their father's words.

"Did you hear me the other times too," Dad asked, wanting to make sure he understood the situation.

"Yes, we heard you every time. We just didn't want to start our chores yet. We were having fun playing. It's not as fun doing chores as it is playing with our toys," Michelle explained to Dad.

Dad sat down on the couch and told his two children to join him. He pulled out his Bible and opened it to the book of James. "Kids, in the New Testament, God tells us that we are not to just hear the Word but we are to do what it says. You disobeyed me by not coming when I called for you, but what's more is that you disobeyed God. Like the Bible says, you heard what I said, but you didn't do it. You were 'hearers' of my words but not 'doers.' When we break rules, we are sinning against God, and that hurts our relationship with him. When our relationship with God is damaged, our relationship with others is also damaged. Living a life for Jesus means obedience, but it also means being careful with your own words and actions. If you aren't you will also not be a do-er."

"But Dad, doesn't the Bible just mean we are to hear and do what the Bible says? It isn't talking about hearing and doing what other people say, is it?" James, who was always looking for a way out of trouble and a way to defend his actions, couldn't get very far with his father.

"James, the Bible isn't just a book of old stories that don't mean anything to us today. The Bible is to be used to help us today in all kinds of situations. If we are wise, we will take what scripture says and try to see how it can help us now. While the verse does say to listen to the Word of God and do what it says, it also teaches children to obey their parents. Because you didn't obey me, neither did you "do" what the Word of God says. You were a 'hearer' only."

"I don't think I like how that sounds. I didn't know it meant that," cried Michelle as a tear streaked her face. "I don't want to hurt you or God, Daddy."

"Me either," James decided. "Next time I'll hear what you say, and I'll do it too. I promise."

Let's Talk About the Story

What does today's memory verse tell us to do?

Did Michelle and James do what it says?

How can you be a doer and not just a hearer of God's Word?

Prayer

Dear Father,

I'm sorry that sometimes we don't listen to you very well. We hear and understand, but we don't do the right thing. Help us to learn to listen and "do" whatever it is we are told. Amen.

Family Activity

Take time this week to find a passage in scripture that your family can put in action such as visiting widows, helping the poor, or giving money to help someone in need. As you do, talk about how this is being a "do-er" of the word, and not a "hearer" only.

References: Proverbs 15: 1; Proverbs 15:23; Colossians 3:23–24; I Thessalonians 4:11–12; I Thessalonians 5:14–15

Week Three–Bold Witness for Christ

Matthew 28:19–20
Therefore go and make disciples of all nations,
baptizing them in the name of the Father and of the Son and
of the Holy Spirit, and teaching them to obey everything
I have commanded you. And surely I am with you always, to
the very end of the age." (NIV)

Go ye therefore, and teach all nations, baptizing them in the
name of the Father, and of the Son, and of the Holy Ghost:
Teaching them to observe all things whatsoever
I have commanded you: and, lo, I am with you always, even
unto the end of the world. (KJV)

Tara, Melanie, and Sheila were in the same class at school. One day when their third grade teacher was on the playground for recess, the three girls were left in the room to do their schoolwork. The teacher had left a small box of candy and a pack of gum sitting on her desk. The girls began to talk about it and how good it looked. It wasn't long before Tara and Melanie were at Mrs. Tillson's desk holding the much longed for items.

"I don't think you should be doing that," said Sheila.

"Why not? We're just looking, we're not hurting anything," the girls responded.

Sheila tried to get back to her work, but Tara and Melanie began to laugh and disturb her. When she looked up, she noticed that they were making fun of her and calling her names for not being a part of what they were doing. Their words and giggles hurt Sheila's feelings. She tried not to cry, but it was hard. She knew they were doing something wrong and she didn't want to be a part of it, but she wanted them to like her. It hurt to feel rejected. It would have been easier to have given in and taken a piece of the gum and candy as they were doing, but she just couldn't. The teacher never seemed to notice anything missing when she came back into the classroom. The rest of the day passed very slowly as Sheila continued to feel rejected from the other two girls in her class. When school was over she walked home a different way so that she could avoid seeing Tara and Melanie. Fortunately she lived near the school so that it didn't take long to get inside where she felt safe.

Sheila's mom greeted her as she walked in. She knew something was wrong with her daughter, so she gave her a hug and asked if she wanted to talk. Before long, Sheila was telling her everything and how badly it made her feel. She also told her mom that she felt like God was mad at her too for not telling her friends that she didn't do that kind of thing because she was a Christian. She began to cry as her mom pulled her close to comfort her. Her mom always seemed to know just the right thing to do to make Sheila feel better. As they talked, her mom told her that being a Christian isn't easy, but she also explained that there are many ways of being a good witness for Christ. Sometimes being a witness means telling people with words that Jesus died for their sins. Other times it means telling them why you don't do certain things. But sometimes, her mom told her, being a bold witness for Christ means doing the right thing and not giving in even when others make fun of you for it.

"Taking a stand for Christ isn't easy, honey. People won't always understand. But we do the right thing because it honors God, not ourselves. You were courageous today when they were making fun of you. I am proud of what you did. You didn't say mean things or make fun of them, even though you may have felt like it. You remained polite. By doing so, you took a stand for Jesus. It may have been a quiet stand to you, but to them, you were loudly telling them that you would not do the same things they were doing because you were different. That took courage!"

"I hadn't thought of it that way. I thought I had to talk about Jesus all the time to be a witness for Him. I feel better now. I guess I am a witness for Jesus even when I don't know I am."

"That's right. God wasn't disappointed in what you did today. He knows how hard it can be, but He will always give you the strength and the courage you need to do the right thing. Always."

Let's Talk About the Story

Who was left alone in the room?
What was on the teacher's desk?
Tell about a time when you have felt like Sheila did?
What does being a bold witness for Jesus mean?

Prayer

Dear Father,
Thank you for teaching me what it means to witness. Thank you for helping me even when I am scared. Help me to be a bold witness for you every day. Amen.

Family Activity

Tell your children about a time when you were afraid to be a bold witness for Christ. Let them know that it is normal for them to feel uneasy. Talk to them about a time when you were rejected because you didn't participate in an activity you knew was wrong.

References: Matthew 10: 32; Romans 1:16; 2 Timothy 1: 12; I Peter 1:15

Week Four—Loving our Enemies

Matthew 6:14–15

For if you forgive men when they sin against you, your heavenly Father will also forgive you. * *But if you do not forgive men their sins, your Father will not forgive your sins. (NIV)*

For if ye forgive men their trespasses, your heavenly Father will also forgive you: * *But if ye forgive not men their trespasses, neither will your Father forgive your trespasses. (KJV)*

As Linda and her two daughters listened to the evening news, a story caught their attention. It was about a man who was arrested after breaking into a house and stealing several things, including a lady's diamond ring that her husband had given to her for their anniversary. Her husband had recently passed away, so the ring was even more special to her. The man was found guilty and put in jail. Mrs. Henley, the owner of the ring, was scared and angry when it first happened. She wanted the burglar, Sam, to pay for his crime and hurt like he had made her hurt.

The news report went on to say that a few weeks after the suspect was caught Mrs. Henley went to visit him in jail. Most people thought that she was going to yell at him and tell him what a horrible thing he had done and how he should feel bad for his crime. Mrs. Henley didn't do that however. Instead, she asked him how he was doing and talked to him in a very calm voice. She told Sam that she had forgiven him for his crime against her and she hoped he was doing well. She also found out that he had a wife and a young daughter at home alone. They didn't have much money for food or clothes and didn't even have a car for transportation so that his wife could work. When Mrs. Henley left, she left with a happy heart and a plan in mind.

The next day Mrs. Henley had an important errand to make. She knocked on the door of a very small house and a little girl opened it looking surprised. Her young mother, poorly dressed, stood close by. Mrs. Henley introduced herself and told her that Sam was concerned about them so she wanted to stop by and see if they were doing all right. Mrs. Henley then handed the young mother some groceries, a few toys for the little girl, and a gift card for the mom so that she could get some new clothes at the store for herself as well. The mother was shocked at what she saw. Without thinking, she hugged Mrs. Henley with tears in her eyes.

"No one has ever been this nice to us before. I don't know what to say."

Mrs. Henley just hugged her back and told her that she wanted her to know that Jesus loved her and she was not angry at Sam anymore. She soon left after giving the mother her phone number and told her she would stop by every week to check on them. Mrs. Henley drove away feeling better than she had felt since her husband had passed away. "Forgiveness is the only way to live," she said as she drove away with a smile on her face.

When the news spot was over, Linda talked to her girls. "Mrs. Henley is right," she said. "Forgiveness is the only way to live. Forgiving someone you love isn't always easy, but it's much easier than forgiving someone you don't know who has hurt you and doesn't seem to care. Mrs. Henley gave us a wonderful example of how to forgive our enemies. We should forgive those who have hurt us because that's what God does for us. Because of Jesus, He forgives all of our sins. Sometimes we may not be able to forgive right away. It may take a long time to be ready to forgive someone if they have hurt us badly, but forgiving others is the only real way to feel peaceful on the inside. Getting back at someone and staying angry never feels as good as the peace we feel when we forgive others for hurting us. Forgiveness is for us, not for them, and we do it because of Jesus."

Linda's girls looked at her and then at each other. They didn't quite understand the whole idea. It seemed too hard to forgive someone like Mrs. Henley had done. But, they knew that what their mom said was right. Forgiveness did seem a better alternative than staying angry.

Let's Talk About the Story

What had happened to Mrs. Henley?

Do you think she ever got the ring back? Do you think she cared about getting it back anymore?

Besides Sam, who did Mrs. Henley go visit?

Do you think Mrs. Henley was a Christian? Why or why not?

Prayer

Dear Father,

Thank you for forgiveness. Help us to forgive people who hurt us and show them your love. Everyone feels better and everyone wins when people forgive rather than staying mad at each other. Amen.

Family Activity

Talk about someone who has hurt you without giving too many details, and tell how you were able to resolve the situation through forgiveness. If possible, schedule a time to visit a jail, prison, or juvenile detention center and talk to the inmates with your kids. Offer to pray for them and ask them if they have any needs that you and your family can meet during the next week.

References: Matthew 5:23–24; Matthew 18:21–22; Ephesians 4:32; Colossians 3:13

May—Who is God?

Suzanne and Robin were having a discussion. Neither one was completely wrong, but neither one was completely right either. The only problem was that they didn't understand that. Suzanne's father heard the arguing and tried to make sense of the girls' misunderstanding.

"Aren't God and Jesus the same person?" argued Suzanne.

"No, they are different, that's why we celebrate Jesus' birth at Christmas time. We say He was God's son, so that must mean that they are two different people," explained Robin.

"I see," said Suzanne's Dad. "It sounds very complicated to me. Let's see if I can help to make it easier to understand. Suzanne, Robin, let's go into the kitchen. I bet some things we have in the kitchen might just be the thing to help us make sense of such a confusing subject."

The girls found the items Mr. Smith was asking for. They found two apples, a small knife to cut an apple with, a boiled egg, and a small bowl. Seeing all these items sure made the girls curious. They couldn't imagine what Mr. Smith was going to do with these things, or how it would help to explain who God and Jesus were. Before long all three were sitting at the kitchen table with a Bible opened. Mr. Smith began to peel one of the apples; then he used the apple corer to take the middle core from it. He set the apple, the core, and the peel in three separate groups and began talking to Robin and Suzanne. "I remember being very confused about this same thing when I was your age, but I think this example will help you as it did me when I was younger.

Mr. Smith held up the unpeeled apple and asked what it was. Rolling their eyes, together they answered, "Duh . . . an apple." Then he held up the peeled apple and asked the same question. Again, the girls responded that it too was an apple even though it looked different. Pointing to the three separate piles, he asked how many parts there were to the apple to which they said, "Three."

"That's right girls. There are three parts to an apple. There are the peel, the core, and the part of the apple that we usually eat," he said as he held up each part. "The apple is three parts in one. Each part is important to the apple, but each is also different and has its own job to do. We call one, '*apple* peel.' One we say is the '*apple* core,' and the other we say is the '*apple* pulp' but they all make up the apple. Does this make sense so far?"

The girls nodded that they understood. He held the whole, unpeeled apple up for them to see and continued, "Just like an apple has three parts but it is still one apple, God has three separate 'parts' to him, but He is still one God. There is God the Father, God the Son, and God the Holy Spirit. We call the 'three- in- one' concept of God the 'Trinity,' which means 'three.' In the same way Suzanne, you are one person but you are my daughter (he held up one finger), you are Robin's best friend (he held up a second finger), and you are a sister (he held up a third finger)," he explained. "God is like that. He is always God and always has been God. That will never change, but He has three different ways that He relates to us. Sometimes God talks to us as the Father. Other times He speaks to us as the Son. And then there are other times that He speaks to us as the Holy Spirit. It is a very hard concept to understand. It's okay if you don't quite understand what the Trinity means. Many adults still don't fully comprehend it. There are many things that we won't understand here on earth, and God knows that. It doesn't make Him angry. But, if we continue following Him and learning about who He is, we will understand some of those things better and better, but we will never get all of it. God is too awesome for us to fully grasp everything about Him."

"Thanks Mr. Smith. That's pretty neat. I do understand it better now than I did when we were arguing about it."

"So, what's the egg for Dad?" asked an inquiring Suzanne.

"Well, the egg is for the same purpose." As he began to crack the egg and peel the shell, he asked the same question. "How many parts make up an egg?"

The girls thought for a moment and then Robin answered, "Three. There's the shell, the white part and the yolk."

"That's right, Robin. Now, Suzanne can you explain to me how the egg is like the Trinity?"

As Suzanne began explaining to him the different parts of the egg, he sliced it into small pieces and passed it around to be shared as a tasty little snack.

Let's Think About God

Who makes up the three "parts" of God?
Are there three Gods, or just one God?
What is the Trinity?

Week One–God the Father

Isaiah 46:9
I am God, and there is no other;* I am God,
and there is none like me. (NIV)

I am God, and there is none else;* I am God,
and there is none like me. (KJV)

"Dad, where's my gym bag?"
"Dad, can you fix my bike?"
"Dad, I need some money."

Mr. Johnson was tired of hearing all the demands and requests from his children. His kids seemed to ask him for everything and needed so much lately. He was worn out. Since his wife had died, he had to handle the kids, his job, and the house all by himself. He never got a break. Yet he loved his children so much, he would do anything for them. As he went to bed one night after an especially long day, his thoughts turned to God. Slowly, he drifted off to sleep until his three-year-old daughter, Claire, awakened him early the next morning. She had been having a bad dream and wanted to crawl in bed with her Daddy to feel safe. All too happily, he drew back the covers and held her close as she snuggled up against him.

The next morning Mr. Johnson felt refreshed. When his oldest son needed money for the field trip, he willingly gave it to him. When his oldest daughter needed her closet door fixed, he patiently went up and repaired it. Then, when Claire came downstairs crying because she couldn't find her favorite doll, he helped her look for it until it was found. His oldest children noticed a difference in their father's mood and commented on the change.

"Gee, what's up with you, Dad," fourteen-year-old Brianna asked.

"Yea, Dad, you're like a different Father," eleven-year-old Cody replied. "You seem more patient this morning. What happened?"

"Last night before I went to sleep, God reminded me that even though my body is getting tired of doing everything a father needs to do for his children, my heavenly father is here to take care of my needs, just as I am here to take care of your needs. Realizing that helped me relax and sleep better than I have in weeks. One difference between God and me though is that our heavenly Father never tires out. He enjoys meeting our needs and finds pleasure in giving us all the things we need. God is a loving father whose patience is unending. When I get impatient and walk away, God reminded me that He never leaves us. He is here by our side every moment of every day."

"Even at night?" asked a still sleepy Claire.

"Yes sweetie, even at night God is still here taking care of us," Daddy said, picking Claire up in his arms.

"Dad, I know that you care when we are sad about Mom

and it hurts you to see us cry, but does God really care about all that? Sometimes it doesn't seem like He does," Brianna quietly said.

"I know what you mean," Daddy began. "Sometimes I feel the same way, but God as our Father cares more for you than I have the capacity to care. His heart hurts deeply when He sees your heart breaking. Whether it's over your mom's death or not getting the part in the school play, God cares. Sometimes when it doesn't feel that way, we just have to trust that it is so."

"Dad," Cody interrupted, "if God is our Father, does He ever want to play with us like you do?"

"I think so, but it's different than when I play with you. God delights in seeing His children having fun just like I do. He finds joy in hearing you laugh with your friends, cheering for the football team and acing the math test. God wants us to tell Him all about our day, the good and the bad." Daddy looked at Claire still in his arms, "God even wants us to tell Him when we're really, really scared. Just as I give you good things to enjoy, God as your Father gives you good things to enjoy too because He wants to see you smile. It makes Him happy."

"I believe that God is our heavenly Father like you said, but I think it's neat that he gave us you here on earth to take care of us. It seems like we can learn a lot about God from watching you. You're doing a good job, Dad," Brianna said as she hugged her dad.

Seconds later, all three children were in a dog pile on the floor with Daddy on the bottom. Squeals and laugher could be heard throughout the house as the Johnson family spent the rest of the morning enjoying each other's company.

Let's Talk About the Story

Why was Mr. Johnson feeling so tired?
What happened to Claire during her sleep?
What did Mr. Johnson tell his kids God was like?

Do you think his kids loved their dad and understood why he was so tired?

Prayer

Dear Father,

It's so good to call you Father. Thank you for being our Heavenly Father who loves us and cares for us. Help us to show others that you are patient, kind, and good. Amen.

Family Activity

During the next week, find some time to point out the different ways God is like a caring Father. At the same time, when you see an earthly father doing something especially kind, explain how that is like God the Father. Make a thank you note for your father or a substitute father you know who has been especially kind to you or your children.

References: Psalm 46:10a; Matthew 7: 9–12; I Peter 1:15; 1 John 4:8; Revelation 1:8

Week Two–God the Son

Hebrews 1:3a
The Son is the radiance of God's glory and the exact representation of his being . . . (NIV)

Who being the brightness of his glory, and the express image of his person . . . (KJV)

John 14:6
Jesus answered, I am the way and the truth and the life. No one comes to the Father except through me. (NIV)

Jesus saith unto him, I am the way, the truth, and the life; no man cometh unto the Father, but by me. (KJV)

"Who is God's son?" six year old Nathan asked his grandfather.

"Jesus is God's son," replied his grandfather.

"Oh, I thought so. Well then, if Jesus is God's son, who is God's daddy? And if you're my grandfather, then who is God's grandfather? Doesn't He have a grandfather like I do? Everybody needs a Paw-paw like you." Nathan was full of questions as he and his grandfather sat on the front porch swing eating cookies and drinking lemonade.

"My," said Nathan's grandfather, "aren't you full of questions today? But since you've done such a good job asking them, I must try my best to answer them just as carefully."

Nathan's grandfather was a preacher and Nathan thought his "Paw-paw" knew everything about God. He loved his Papa more than almost anyone. They had a very special bond and enjoyed being together as often as they could.

"Nathan, God sent Jesus to this world as a baby in a manger over 2,000 years ago. Jesus is another name for God. They are the same person, but they have different jobs to do. When God wanted to come to earth as a person, He needed to think of a really creative way to do it. Everyone expected Him to come as a powerful king, but God didn't want to come that way. He wanted to come as a very innocent, sweet baby and in a way that no one would expect. He took on a new name when He came as a human being; that was the name Jesus, or Emmanuel which means 'God is with us.' It was such a special occasion the night He was born in Bethlehem that we still celebrate it today. That's what Christmas is all about—celebrating God's presence as a person, in the form of Baby Jesus. But God didn't need another son or even a daughter. Jesus met all the needs we had. In the same way, God didn't need a father either. I know you and I need our daddies, or at least I did when I was a young boy, but God is different. He isn't a person the way we think of people as being. He is spiritual, which means He has no beginning and no end. He doesn't need sleep, or food, or water. That's hard to grasp, I know. Even adults have a hard time understanding anything that has no beginning and no end. But that's just how God is. God has always been God and He will forever and ever always be God. Because of that, He didn't need a daddy to tuck Him in at night, read Him a story, have tickle fights or teach Him how to play baseball. He made us to need daddies and daddies to need children, but God had no need for His own father. God didn't need a grandfather either for the same reason. Believe it or not, God didn't need ice cream and big bear hugs and evenings on porch swings. He is so awesome and powerful, He didn't need anyone before Him."

"So, that's why God doesn't have a daddy or a grand-father the way we do, because He doesn't need one?" asked a confused Nathan.

"That's right, see how fast you learn."

"Paw-paw, that's confusing," I don't think I will ever understand it," Nathan declared as he jumped off the swing and ran to get the evening newspaper.

"In time, I'm sure you will understand it better. No one understands everything about God, not even an old preacher like your grandfather. It takes a lifetime of loving God to get as close as we can though."

"I think all I can remember is that Jesus is God's son like Daddy is your son and I'm his son. That makes sense to me."

"I'm glad that part makes sense to you and for now, that's good enough. But will you do me a favor?"

"Sure, what's that?"

"Whenever you do understand it, will you explain it to me?"

Let's Talk About the Story

Where were Nathan and his grandfather sitting?
What questions did Nathan ask his grandfather?
Can you tell who Jesus is and why God didn't need a grandfather?

Prayer

Dear Father,

Thank you for being our father and for sending Jesus as your son. It can sure be confusing though. Help us to understand your plan more and more as we grow in you. Amen.

Family Activity

Sit around the floor one evening and talk about some special memories that you have of your parents when you were growing up. Have them tell about some favorite memories of their grandparents or even of you.

References: Matthew 1:21, 23; John 1:1–4; John 10; John 11:25; Acts 4:12; 2 Corinthians 5:2; Philippians 2: 6–11; Colossians 1:15–20; Colossians. 2:9; Hebrews 13:8; Revelation 1:13–17

Week Three–God, the Holy Spirit

John 14:26

But the Counselor, the Holy Spirit, whom the Father will send in my name, will teach you all things* and will remind you of everything I have said to you. (NIV)

But the Comforter, which is the Holy Ghost, whom the Father will send in my name, he shall teach you all things,* and bring all things to your remembrance, whatsoever I have said unto you. (KJV)

Who is the Holy Spirit? Many children want to know the answer to that question and are confused by what they hear. You probably hear more about God, and Jesus, God's son, than you do about the Holy Spirit. Learning all the different ways God shows Himself can be hard to remember and understand. That's okay though, even adults have a hard time keeping it straight.

The scripture memory verse for this week gives you a hint at who the Holy Spirit is and what He does. First of all, God's spirit, the Holy Spirit, is holy because God is holy. That's why we call Him the "Holy Spirit." Because it is another name for God and what He does, we use capital letters for His name. Instead of spelling it "holy spirit," we spell it, "Holy Spirit", with capital letters to show respect and honor. Just like your first and last name is always written with a capital letter so is His. And, because there is only one spirit of God, not two or three or even more, we use the word "The" in front of it to let people know that there is one true spirit. Another important fact to remember is that because the Bible always refers to God with "He" or "Him," and because Jesus was a boy and then a man, the Holy Spirit is also referred to with "He," "Him," or "His" since He is a reflection of God. We do not call the Holy Spirit of God "it" for the same reason we don't call you "it"; you deserve to be called either "she" or "he" and so does the Holy Spirit.

Those are some of the basic aspects of the Holy Spirit, but we still don't know what He does or why He is a part of us. Let's talk about that now. The Bible tells us that the Holy Spirit was sent to be a helper and a comforter for us after Jesus left the earth for heaven. Just like your mom or dad comforts you and makes you feel better when you are sad, the Holy Spirit does the same thing. In fact that is His main purpose. He is our comforter. Do you have a favorite doll or blanket that makes you feel better whenever you hold it close, or a music CD that brings you comfort every time you listen to it? Do you remember how it felt the last time you were sick to crawl under your soft, warm covers in your bed? The Holy Spirit is not a blanket or doll, but in the same way you might look to those things to bring you a happy or peaceful feeling, God's Spirit brings us comfort in much the same way. We can relax in God's love and comfort just as if we were holding our favorite doll, listening to our favorite music, or sleeping in Mom and Daddy's big, warm bed. Now that's comfort!

The Holy Spirit has other jobs to do too, being our "comforter" is just one of them, but it's a very important one.

Let's Talk About the Story

Who is the Holy Spirit?
Why do we call Him holy?
Whose spirit is it?
What is the purpose of the Holy Spirit in our lives?

Prayer

Dear Father,

Thank you for sending us your Holy Spirit to comfort us when we are sad, or scared, or lonely. Thank you for caring so much for us that you want to comfort us. Help us to comfort other people the way your spirit comforts us. Amen.

Family Activity

During this next week, bring out favorite dolls, toys, and blankets and talk about the feelings they bring. If your kids are older now, bring out their old favorites and enjoy reminiscing about the times these special items brought comfort to them. You might also have a pajama night where everyone gets in their pajamas early, then play games, read books, sit by the fire place, drink hot chocolate, listen to favorite music or even crawl in your bed together and talk about how comforting all these things can be. Discuss how the Holy Spirit operates in much the same way in our own lives, bringing comfort to us when we are sad, hurting, or disappointed.

References: John 14:15–17; Romans 8:26; Ephesians 1:13–14; Ephesians 4:30; I Corinthians 3:16; Galatians 5:22–25

Week Four–The Many Qualities of God

I Peter 1:15–16
But just as he who called you is holy, so be holy in all you do;
for it is written: "Be holy, because I am holy."(NIV)

But as he which hath called you is holy, so be ye holy in all
manner of conversation; because it is written, Be ye holy; for
I am holy. (KJV)

"Mom, why is it so hard to understand who God is? If He wants us to follow Him, shouldn't He have made it easier to understand?"

"I think that's a great question, Jacalyn," Mom replied. "But tell me, what is the hardest part in understanding God right now?"

"He just seems so big and like He's faraway. You and Dad talk about Him like He's real and living in this house like a friend or something, but He doesn't seem that way to me. How can I make Him feel like someone living next door or even in the same house with me?"

Nine-year-old Jacalyn had a good point and some very good questions. Sometimes it is hard to understand God. It's not God's fault; it's because we are so much smaller than He is and He is so much wiser that it is hard for people to understand everything about who He is. That doesn't mean we give up and quit trying however. It means we keep on trying and learning more about Him until we are with Him in heaven. Everyday should be spent getting to know more about God.

"Jacalyn, one reason God seems distant to some people is because of how they think of Him," Mom began explaining. "If you think of Him as wanting to be your best friend, you will spend more time with Him. If you think of Him as being a stranger who doesn't care, you will not want to get to know Him better. God has many qualities that would draw anyone to Him if they only took the time to discover who He is. The Bible tells us about those qualities, or attributes, so that we might know who He is. If we were to describe our best friend, we might start by saying how nice she is, or how funny he is. We might say that she is very giving, thoughtful, or kind. Another way that we could describe a friend is to say that he is smart, unselfish, or likes to help other people. Of course no one has all of the qualities that we could list, but God does.

"We know from the memory verse this week that God is Holy. That means He is set-apart. He is set apart from sin and evil. But God isn't just holy. He is much more than that. Like any good friend, God is kind, forgiving, patient, and generous. He is understanding too. If we make a mistake, He understands and forgives us. He doesn't stay mad at us like we might if a friend had hurt us. We also know that God is wise. Being wise means more than just being smart. Being smart means that someone knows a lot of things, but being wise means you know the right thing to do and you do it. God is certainly smart, but more than that, He is wise." Mother brushed back Jacalyn's long dark hair and rubbed her cheeks with her hand. "He is also faithful and honest. The Bible tells us that God cannot lie. It is impossible for Him to lie because He is Truth. But I think one of the biggest attributes of God is that He is love. *God is love.* Without God loving us first, we wouldn't even know how to love anybody but ourselves. It is because of God's great love that we can love others no matter who they are. God made every single person and He loves what He made. He loves all of His creation because He *is love.*"

Jacalyn looked at her mom who had gotten up to pour some milk. "Now that you know more about who God is, if you try to think about Him like He is your best friend or neighbor you might find that soon you are talking about Him as Daddy and I do, like He is right here with us, because to us He is. He is a friend that is always with us."

Mom finished talking to Jacalyn and sat down with her daughter to have a class of milk. It was almost time for dance class, and they didn't want to be late. They could finish the conversation later if Jacalyn wanted to, but for now, she's learned a lot about God and what makes Him such a wonderful friend.

Let's Talk About the Story

What was Jacalyn confused about?
Do you think her mom helped her understand?
Name three things that describe God.
Do you have a best friend? Tell about your friend and why you like him or her.

Prayer

Dear Father,
We are learning so much about you. Thank you for showing us who you are through your son Jesus. Thank you for wanting us to have a real relationship with you. Help us to tell others what an awesome friend you are. Amen.

Family Activity

Try to find pictures of times when the children were having fun with a friend. Talk about what made that time so much fun and why they liked that friend. Talk about the many attributes of God and how He too wants to be our friend.

References: Joshua 1:5; Psalm 103:8–13, 17; Psalm 107:1; Isaiah 9:6; I Peter 5:7; I John 4:8

June—Respecting Others

During this month, you will be learning about the importance of respecting people of all different ages, and backgrounds. The word respect simply means to show another person consideration, or kindness, for who they are or what they do. You don't have to always agree with people, or even like them, but according to God's Word, as followers of Jesus, we must show respect to everyone without being rude. Many times that is hard to do because our feelings get in the way of doing what is right. We may not like someone very much or we may be angry at them, or we may feel that they didn't respect us once so we won't show respect to them. But regardless of our feelings or past experiences, we are to be considerate of everyone, even if it means doing what we really don't want to do at the time. Don't worry if you don't understand it all right now, it will make more sense to you as you go through the stories. Respecting others is a good thing that we are commanded to do, not a bad thing. And, once we show respect to other people, they usually begin showing respect to us, too. That makes us feel really good!

As children, you are commanded by God to show respect to your parents. But did you know that even your parents are commanded to show respect to people, too? Even when they don't feel like it, parents must demonstrate an attitude of respect towards people. This month, see how many groups of people we are told to respect as you hear the stories and memorize the Bible verses that go along with each story. As you begin to understand more about how God expects us to relate to others, see if there is an area of respect that God would want you to work on. God knows it's not easy to respect everyone all the time. He knows you'll forget from time to time. That's okay though because he'll help you as you try to follow him. Just ask him!

Let's Think About Respect

Do you know what "respect" means?

Who promises to always help you when it's hard to show respect to someone?

As you learn about respect this month, think about ways that you can show respect to God as well as others in your life.

Week One—Respecting Parents

Ephesians 6:1
Children, obey your parents in the Lord:
for this is right. (NIV)

Children, obey your parents in the Lord,
for this is right. (KJV)

"Jack," Dad called from the living room, "time for homework. Play time is over."

Dad gave seven year-old Jack plenty of time to stop the video game and begin his weekly spelling homework before he went to his room to check on his progress. When he got to the door, he noticed that Jack was still playing his game. Quickly Dad turned the television off and looked straight at his son's eyes.

UH-OH! Somehow Jack knew he was in big trouble now. Didn't Dad understand how important this game was, not to mention how much fun it was to play, he thought to himself. "But, but, Dad! I was just finishing."

"Jack, how many times do we have to tell you to do something the first time we give instructions? I'm sorry, but I have to ground you from video games for the rest of the week. Now start your homework and we'll talk when you're finished." Jack knew how to do his homework all by himself. It wasn't too hard for him. He just didn't feel like doing it.

When he had finished his spelling, he brought it to his mom to check and then put it in his backpack for school the next morning. Afterwards, Mom and Dad both sat down to talk with their son. "Jack, we love you, but we need you to understand how important it is for you to listen and respect us. Learning to respect your parents is a big part of growing up. It's not always easy, but it is something that God requires of His children."

"It's just that I don't like doing my homework every night, and I really was almost finished with the game. I was going to start my homework after that," Jack argued.

"Honey, the important thing isn't doing what you want to do, it's in doing what we have instructed you to do, whether you want to or not." Dad had a way of saying things that seven year-old Jack couldn't ignore. He knew he had better listen to what his parents were saying now.

Dad continued, "God has given us the privilege and the responsibility of raising you in a way that brings glory to Jesus. The Bible tells children that they are to obey their parents. It makes God very happy when children obey without arguing, fussing, or stalling. Learning to obey is part of what respect is all about."

"Jack, when you disobey, you have to be punished for your actions. Hopefully the punishment will help you remember to obey the next time a similar situation arises when you'd rather do your own thing instead of what you are told."

"By the way, son," Mom's voice was calm and soothing. "Did you know that parents are also given a command by God? In the book of Ephesians, fathers are told not to 'exasperate' or irritate their children unnecessarily, but to raise them up in the ways of the Lord. We also have to respect God and make sure that we do what He requires of us. That's not always easy for us either."

"I know I disobeyed you, and I'm sorry I didn't do what you said, Dad. Will you forgive me for not obeying?" Jack felt bad for his actions earlier in the evening. He had learned a big lesson about respecting parents and what God expects of him.

"Sure son, I love you." With that Dad gave Jack a big bear hug before throwing him on the floor for a tickle fight.

"Ahh! Help, Mom!" Laughter once again filled the home as father and son pounced and squirmed around the room before saying good-night for the evening.

Let's Talk About the Story

What did Jack's father tell him to do?

How did Jack feel about it?

Have you ever been told to do something by your parents that you didn't really want to do? Talk about what happened.

What does the Bible tell children to do?

Prayer

Dear Heavenly Father,

I know you want us to obey our parents, but sometimes that sure is hard to do. Sometimes I just don't feel like it. Help me to respect my mom and dad by obeying them everyday. Will you forgive me for disobeying them? Thank you for my parents. I love you God. Amen.

Family Activity

Take some time this week to tell your children about the consequences you experienced when you didn't obey your parents as a child. Tell them about times when you still must obey and show respect to them even though you are grown. Ask them how they would feel if they were in charge of a younger child who wouldn't obey. Talk about those times that are the hardest for them to show respect towards you and how they can better handle the situation before it is a problem.

References: Exodus 20:12; Leviticus 19:3

Week Two–Respecting Authority

Romans 13:1
[Everyone must submit himself to the governing authority,]
for there is no authority except that which God
has established. . . . (NIV)

[Let every soul be subject unto the higher powers.]
For there is no power but of God; the powers that be are
ordained of God. (KJV)

"Mom, why do we have to do what grown-ups say, even when they're wrong? It doesn't seem right to me." Eleven-year-old Jessica had a few questions about respecting other people.

"What makes you ask a question like that, Jessica?" Mom gently responded.

"Well in Sunday School we've been learning about obeying and respecting grown-ups. It sounds easy in church, but sometimes at school it is really hard to do."

Mom knew there was more to Jessica's story than what she had shared so far, so she inquired further, "Is there a teacher at school that you are having a problem with, sweetheart?"

"Well, kind of," confided her daughter. "It's Mrs. Gibson. She is always picking on us in class. Madelyn, Vanessa, and I are always getting in trouble for nothing. When we try to explain, she just ignores us and tells us to stop arguing. I don't even want to go back to her class again."

"Jessica, sometimes adults are wrong in what we say. Sometimes we are wrong in the things that we do. Grown-ups aren't perfect. We are people and people of every age make mistakes because of sin. It doesn't make it right though."

"So, if you are wrong, then why do kids still have to be respectful?"

"Jessica, God's Word tells us very clearly that as Christians we are to submit to everyone in authority over us. 'Submit' means to obey, or follow someone. The word 'authority' means someone who is in charge of something. We believe that God is the final authority, but He has placed others over us in a set order. God knows when those leaders are being unfair. He may not change the situation, but He will always help you learn to handle the situation better."

"You mean even when we don't like someone, we still have to be nice and respectful?"

"That's right. You won't always like the leaders placed over you, but it is important to learn to respect them nonetheless. Right now it may be a teacher; later it could be your boss at work, or even the president of the United States. It doesn't matter what position they hold, God expects you to treat them with consideration, as if it were the Lord that you were working for."

Mom continued, "You may not agree with them, but somewhere deep, deep down, we all have to learn to treat others with respect, even if we don't respect what they do. Sometimes people won't deserve the respect given them, but if we keep in mind how much God loves them, and know that He is in control, it makes it easier. Many times, a person who acts "mean" is really sad on the inside and it causes them to act that way."

With a smile, Jessica reached out to hug her mom. "Thanks Mom, I guess I understand better now, but I still don't like it."

"Hey Jessica, how about if you help me bake some cookies tonight? You can take some to Mrs. Gibson tomorrow. I'll send a note with it, thanking her for the time and effort she puts in to teaching. Maybe she feels unappreciated for all of her hard work?" Mom's thoughts seemed to make sense to Jessica.

"Well, okay, but only if I can eat some of the cookie dough!" With that, both Jessica and Mom headed for the kitchen where lots of laughter and love filled the room the rest of the evening.

Let's Talk About the Story

Who was Jessica having a problem with?
Did she want to do what Mom told her to do?
Who does the Bible say we are to show respect towards?

Prayer

Dear God,

I am learning about showing respect towards others, even when I don't want too. You give me a lot of things that I don't deserve; help me to give others respect, even when they don't deserve it. I love you, God. Amen.

Family Activity

This week when you hear your child complain about someone, remember to pray aloud for that person and for your child's attitude towards him or her. Ask them to "catch" you when you are being disrespectful towards another, and then pray for the other person too.

References: Romans 13:1–5; Titus 3:1–2; 1 Peter 2:13; 1 Peter 2:17

Week Three–Respecting Your Elders

Leviticus 19:32
"Rise in the presence of the aged, show respect for the elderly* and revere your God. I am the LORD." (NIV)

"Thou shalt rise up before the hoary head, and honour the face of the old man,* and fear thy God; I am the LORD." (KJV)

"Joshua, are all your belongings packed? It's almost time to leave now."

"Yes, Ma'am everything is packed, but I don't want to go yet. I want to stay longer." Joshua knew the week long visit to his grandparents' house was coming to a close, but he sure wasn't looking forward to saying good-bye. Every summer since turning five, he got to visit his grandparents for a whole week without his younger brother and sister. They were okay as far as brothers and sisters go, but sometimes it was nice to be alone, and this was one of those times.

"It sure has been nice having you here with us all week. I look forward to this time each year, Joshua." Grandma's pleasant voice and long hug felt good.

Before he knew it, the time had come to load up the car and head for home. On the way back, Joshua and Grandpa talked about all the great things they had done together the past week. Grandpa also led the three of them in singing funny songs to make the time pass faster as they traveled along the highway. Even the trip home was fun with Grandma and Grandpa.

That night as he lay in his own warm bed his thoughts returned to all the adventures he had experienced over the past seven days.

"Mama, Grandma and Grandpa are really fun. I love going to their house. I'm glad you and Daddy let me go."

"Well, Joshua, we're glad you enjoy it so much. You are very fortunate to have such wonderful grandparents. Some children never get to know theirs. Can you imagine never having grandparents to visit or never being able to sit in their laps and listen to stories?"

"That would be VERY sad, Mama. I love Grandma and Grandpa."

"Joshua, did you know that the Bible tells us to love older people like Grandma and Grandpa? Older people are known as seniors, one's "elders" or "the elderly."

In the Old Testament, we are instructed to treat the elderly with great respect. It even says that we should stand in their presence, giving them honor. We show respect to our elders in many different ways: by giving them our seat, even if we must remain standing; holding doors open for them, using proper language and manners around them, and listening to what they have to say. Some people don't understand the love of older people and what it means to respect them. They treat them rudely, and say mean things about them."

"Maybe that's because they never had grandparents to love them like we do, Mom." Joshua was trying to understand how people could treat older people in a mean way. It just didn't make much sense to him.

"You're probably right, son. Whenever you see someone being rude to an older person, maybe you could tell them how special older people are to you, like your own grandparents."

"Okay, but for right now I think I want to go to sleep and dream about all the fun things we did this week."

Let's Talk About the Story

Where had Joshua been for a whole week?

Who does God say we are to respect?

What should you do if you see someone treating an older person with disrespect?

Why do you think some people treat others with no respect?

Prayer

Dear God,

Thank you for my grandparents and all the fun we have when we are together. Please help me show others how to respect older people when they are being rude to them. You're idea of grandparents sure was a good idea! Thanks God. I love you. Amen.

Family Activity

Find some time this week to help your children write a

letter of love to their grandparents. If your children are too small to do this themselves, you can write down what they say and have them draw a picture to send with it. You might also make time for them to take their grandparents out on a special "date" with you as a way of saying "thank you." If grandparents don't live nearby, consider adopting grandparents from your neighborhood or church, or visiting a nursing home nearby. This could become a permanent arrangement with wonderful benefits for all parties involved.

References: 1 Thessalonians 5:12–13; Hebrews 13:17

Week Four–Respecting Your Peers

1 Peter 2:17
Show proper respect to everyone: Love the brotherhood of believers, fear God, honor the king. (NIV)*

Honour all men. Love the brotherhood. Fear God. Honour the king. (KJV)*

Usually four-year-old Brooke was an adorable and charming little girl. Today, however, she was having a bad day. Even at four, life can be hard. The way she saw it, nothing seemed to be going her way. Her best friend, Emily was invited to go to another friend's house to play after preschool. Her big brother got a free pizza award from school, and worst of all, she had to clean her room all by herself. Needless to say, she was not easy to be around. In fact, neither of her brothers felt like being very nice to her at all, the way she was acting.

In the car, Brooke didn't like the funny noises the two boys were making. When her mom put in a CD to listen to, Brooke demanded another one be put in instead. She even hit her oldest brother when he accidentally bumped her while putting on his seat belt. Her brothers decided if this was how Brooke was going to act, then they would treat her the same way. It wasn't long before yelling, squealing, and arguing erupted in the car from all seats. Mom pulled the car over to the side of the road, turned around and began her "mommy talk." They never liked this part of the punishment. Mom had a way of talking to them that got their attention and made them feel uncomfortable, without even raising her voice!

"Boys," Mom began, "I know Brooke isn't being very nice to anyone right now. She is having a very hard day. And even though that doesn't excuse her actions, it might help if you would try understanding why she is acting so differently today."

"But, Mom, she isn't even being fair! Why should we try to understand her when she is acting like this?"

"That's a good question, Benjamin. I know you're angry at her, but I believe the answer is found in the Bible. It's called 'respect' and it is how God wants us to treat everyone, whether they are being nice or not. Jesus treated everyone He met with respect, even when they were accusing Him of all sorts of lies. Jesus is our role model. We should try to make our life copy His as much as possible, even when it seems impossible or unfair."

"She doesn't deserve us to be nice to her, Mama. All she is doing is fighting and crying!" exclaimed Nicholas.

"Nicholas, people won't always deserve the respect we give them. That doesn't matter though. We are told to show proper respect to everyone. You may not like what they are doing, but you do need to find a nice way to respond even when you don't like their behavior."

"Mama, does that mean at school too, or just at home? Do we have to be 'respectful' even when you and Daddy aren't around?"

"Benjamin, that means wherever you are and whoever you are with—friends, strangers, family members, and even moreso if they are Christians. Respect isn't easy to give, and others won't always deserve it, but that is what God expects of us, nonetheless. Even to sisters who are having a bad day."

Both boys listened carefully to everything mom had said. They knew at times that they were also hard to be around. They knew that Mom was right, and they would just have to find a way to be nicer to their sister, even though she certainly didn't deserve it. It wouldn't be long before she would be back to her fun, silly self again anyway.

"Hey, Brooke, do you want me to read my new book to you. I just checked it out of the library today."

Let's Talk About the Story

Who was having a bad day?

Why was she so upset?

What did Mom say Benjamin and Nicholas should do?

What is one thing you could do when someone you know is having a bad day?

Prayer

Dear Heavenly Father,

Thank you for always showing respect to us, even when we don't deserve it. Help me to be respectful of my friends too. Thank you for friends and sisters. I love you God. Amen.

Family Activity

Make a type of game out of "respect" this week. Put everyone's name in a "hat" and have each person draw one name. That person will be their "project" all week as they try to show respect in a special way to him or her each day. At the end of the week, talk about what they have learned. Ask how it felt to be the one receiving respect, as well as giving it.

References: Romans 12:10; Romans 14:1; Romans 14:13; Romans 15:7; 1 Thessalonians 5:12–13; James 2:1

July—Christian Basics, "What, Why, and How?"

Patrick had many questions about church, the Bible and God. He and his family had just started going to church a few months ago so no one in his family knew how to answer his questions very well. He wanted to know everything he could about Christianity and so did his parents. One night as he was finishing supper, there was a knock at the door. He heard his dad open the door and begin visiting with someone. Patrick didn't recognize the voice so he went to see who it was. It was Brother Mike, the pastor at their church. He could tell that his dad was enjoying the visit as they sat down in the living room to continue the conversation. Mother brought in some coffee and soon all three were visiting and laughing. When Mother saw Patrick watching from the stairs, she motioned for him to come join them. Patrick was the oldest of four children and the most curious about church. The other children were occupied in their rooms, so he decided to go sit down by his dad and listen in on the conversation with their pastor. It wasn't long before the pastor asked if they had any questions that he could answer for them. Twelve-year-old Patrick's face lit up; this was his chance to get some answers to the questions that had been bothering him for so long. His mom and dad had the same questions and many more; hopefully they would let him ask his first.

In no time, Patrick was intently listening as Brother Mike patiently answered his questions. He asked about church, prayer, the Bible, faith, sin, healing, and dying. The pastor used scripture to give answers to his questions so Patrick knew he wasn't making up answers as he thought of them. That gave him confidence to know that Brother Mike really cared and knew the

Bible very well. He liked his new pastor and could tell that his parents did too. In the end, Patrick understood things better, but more importantly, he had learned that he could read the Bible for himself to find answers to questions that came up each day. He didn't have to wait to ask a preacher; God would show him the answers too. Brother Bob taught Patrick and his parents how to search the scripture for answers and then gave them his phone number. He told them to call anytime they needed to ask another question. As Patrick learned, there's more to learning about God than just getting a few questions answered, but he was on his way. With the help of his parents, his Sunday School teachers, and now his pastor, it wouldn't be long before Patrick would be answering other people's questions.

Let's Think About Christianity

Why did Patrick and his parent's not know much about the Bible?

Who stopped by for a visit one evening?

What did Patrick learn about studying God's Word?

Week One–Does God Hear Me When I Pray?

Matthew 7:7–8

Ask and it will be given to you; seek and you will find; knock and the door will be opened to you. For everyone who asks receives; he who seeks finds; and to him who knocks, the door will be opened. (NIV)

Ask, and it shall be given you; seek, and ye shall find; knock, and it shall be opened unto you. (KJV)

Landon Roberts had been a Christian for only a few months. He was reading his Bible every day and going to church whenever he could. He had learned a lot about Christianity, but there was still so much he didn't understand. He finally decided to call his pastor, Brother Mike, and get some answers from him. He dialed the phone number. When Janette, the church secretary, answered, she put his fears to rest. Brother Mike quickly picked up the phone in his office and sounded thrilled to hear Landon on the other end.

"Landon, it's great to hear your voice. I haven't heard from you in a while. What can I do for you?"

Landon told him how he had taken the challenge to read the Bible for himself and seek out the answers to his questions from scriptures. He told him how much he had learned in just the past month and how excited it made him feel. Finally, he told Brother Mike that he had a few questions he couldn't figure out and needed his help. Of course, Brother Mike was more than happy to help, and so Landon began asking his questions over the phone that afternoon to his new friend and pastor.

"Bro. Mike, I was wondering how God hears us when we pray when He is so far away. I also wanted to know why God doesn't answer all of my prayers. I thought that if we prayed, He would answer us. Isn't that what the Bible tells us?"

"Landon, those are some great questions. Let's start by addressing the first question that so many people have. The reason God hears us when we pray is because He isn't far away at all. Through the Holy Spirit, God lives within each of us when we ask Him into our hearts. We may think of God as only living in heaven, but the truth is that God is spirit and His Spirit is all around us. He is everywhere all at the same time filling His creation with His presence. God is not bound to heaven or to one place as we are because He is not a person. That's why He is as close as a prayer. And that's also why you can pray at anytime, in any location and He will hear you. It doesn't matter how you pray—if you sit or stand. You can pray out loud or silently. You can kneel by your bed, pray at school before a big test, or pray on the football field. God hears every prayer.

"As far as God not answering your prayers . . . well, the truth is that God does answer your prayers—all of them. Sometimes it may not seem like He hears us because we are expecting Him to answer our way. If He answers in a way that is different than we were expecting, we may not realize He has even answered because we were looking for a different answer. Just like your parents don't always respond to your requests in the way you'd like, God might not either, but that doesn't mean He isn't answering. Your parents may tell you 'no,' or they could say 'yes.' They might even say 'not now,' or 'wait.' Those are hard answers to hear but they are still answers. God is the same way. He only wants to give us what is best and sometimes the best thing for us is not what we ask for, but something better. So, if your question is really, 'Why does God not answer my prayers the way I want?' That's because we don't always know what is best for us. If your question is, 'Does God always answer my prayers?' Then the answer is absolutely yes. We can be confident of that. Landon, God wants us to talk to Him as if we were speaking to our earthly father or our best friend. He wants us to pray in order to develop our relationship with Him and learn to trust Him. Prayer encourages us, it gives us strength, it helps other people and most of all, it pleases God. I hope that helps explain what prayer is, why we practice it and how important it is to the life of a believer."

"It does help. Thanks for your time Brother Mike. I better let you go now. I have a lot of praying to do." With that Landon hung up the phone and headed to his room where he spent the next few moments talking to God.

Let's Talk About the Story

What were Landon's questions about prayer?
What did his pastor tell him?
Does it matter where or how we pray?
Why is it important to spend time praying?

Prayer

Dear Father,

Thank you for teaching us about prayer. Thank you for caring so much about us that you don't always give us everything we ask for. Help us to trust you more and know that you only want what's best for us. Amen.

Family Activity

During the week keep record of how often your answers to your children's request are "yes." Compare this to how God answers our prayers. Record your family prayer requests and write down God's answers as they become evident.

References: Psalm 139: 23–24; Philippians 4:19; I John 5:14–15

Week Two–What is the Bible?

Psalm 119: 105
Your word is a lamp to my feet and a light for my path. (NIV)

Thy word is a lamp unto my feet,
and a light unto my path. (KJV)

Psalm 119:11
I have hidden your word in my heart that I
might not sin against you. (NIV)

Thy word have I hid in mine heart, that I might not
sin against thee. (KJV)

It was 6:00 A.M. Mrs. Ross quietly got out of bed, put on her robe and slippers and poured a glass of orange juice, her favorite morning drink. As she made her way to the sofa, all was quiet in the house except for the sweet purr of Miss Charity, the family cat, who had hopped up on the sofa next to her as if to say "good morning." The sun was just peeking through the clouds. It was a very peaceful morning. Mrs. Ross usually awoke before her husband and two sons so that she could enjoy the quiet and spend time with the Lord. As she opened up her Bible to read from the book of Psalms, she heard the pitter-patter of little feet coming down the hall. It was her five-year-old son, Joshua. Sleepy eyed and cold, she let him crawl in her lap and snuggle underneath the warm blanket she had thrown over her legs. Mrs. Ross kissed her oldest child on the cheek, held him close, then began reading God's Word. After she was finished reading, she closed her Bible to think about what she had just read.

"Mommy, what were you doing? Joshua inquired.

"I was reading my Bible" she responded.

"Why were you doing that? It's not Sunday is it?"

"No, honey it's not. Today is Thursday, but I always like to try and read my Bible everyday."

"Why do you want to do that? Don't you know all the stories in it by now? I already know most of them, and I'm only five" said a proud Joshua.

Smiling, his mother answered, "The Bible is God's Word. If we don't spend time reading it during the week, we won't know what God wants to teach us. God's Word is a very special book. It has all sorts of things for us to learn, including the stories you love so much. God's Word is like a very special letter to us. When you received the letter from your grandmother last week you treasured it and read it over and over. Then you found a very safe place to keep it. Right? Well, that's how the Bible is to those that love God. We want to keep it close to our hearts and read it over and over again. And when we memorize verses, it's like we are hiding them in the secret places of our hearts, so that we can always know right where to find a special thought from God just when we need it."

"Is that why you and Daddy and my Sunday School

teachers want us to 'member Bible verses? So we can hide them in our heart and never forget them no matter where we are?"

"That's exactly right. But not only that, we want you to know God's word so that you can know God better. Your daddy and I look to God's Word for direction in raising you and your brother and sister, for help when we are sad, and to help us be strong when we don't feel so strong on the inside. The Bible gives us help for many different times in our lives, but if we don't know what it says, it can't help us very much. God told some very special chosen men a long, long time ago to write down what He whispered in their hearts so that others would know how to live a life that would be pleasing to Him and would know right from wrong. Because of that, we have the Bible today.

"God's Word is perfect. It has been around for thousands of years, longer than Grandma and Grandpa and even their parents! It will continue to stay with people forever. That is God's plan. Since it is perfect and right and has been around for so many years, we know that we can trust what it says. After all, it is God's Word and God doesn't ever lie."

Joshua wriggled under the blanket and thought for a moment. Finally he said, "I love Jesus and I want to do what He says, but I don't know how to read all those big words yet. Is God mad at me for not reading my Bible everyday like you do?"

Mrs. Ross hugged her son tightly then looked into his blue eyes and said, "Of course not, son. God doesn't expect anyone to do something they can't do yet. He understands. But as your parents, it is our responsibility to help you learn about God and to read the Bible to you like we do with our family devotions. We are following God's command when we do that."

With that, Joshua snuggled closer to his mom and pulled the blanket up around his shoulders and closed his eyes. Mrs. Ross silently thanked God for His Word, the Bible, then laid her head back gently as she watched her son doze off to sleep.

Let's Talk About the Story

Why did Mrs. Ross wake up early every morning?

Why is it important to read the Bible?

Will God be disappointed if you don't read the Bible every day?

What can you do to show God that you love him?

Prayer

Dear Father,

Thank you for giving us your Word, the Bible. Help us to follow it every day. Help us to understand it even when it seems hard. We love you God. Amen.

Family Activities

Plan a time when your family can take a night walk in the neighborhood using flashlights. Turn them off and talk about how dark it is without light to guide you. Then, turn them back on and see how much brighter it looks. Point out that with light to guide you; you can see the path in front to know where your foot should step and which way is the right way to go. Without the light, it is much more dangerous and uncertain about where to go. Relate this to scripture as being our light and the "lamp unto my feet."

References: Proverbs 8:10; Isaiah 40:8; Isaiah 55:11–12; Ephesians 6:10–11; 2 Timothy 3:16–17; Hebrews 4:12

Week Three–Church . . . Again?

Psalm 122: 1

I rejoiced with those who said to me, "Let us go to the house of the Lord." (NIV)

I was glad when they said unto me, Let us go into the house of the Lord." (KJV)

Eight-year-old Jordan ran in the house and handed his mother an invitation to a birthday party. He had already heard all about it and couldn't wait to go. As his mother read the date and time, she got a sad look on her face.

"What's wrong, Mom? I can go, can't I? It's Matt's party."

Mom thought a minute and then said, "Jordan, did you read the invitation before you handed it to me?"

"No, ma'am, I was too excited. I just handed it to you without looking at it, 'cause I knew what it was. Matt told me," replied Jordan in a very confident voice.

"Jordan, the party is on the 16th, which is next weekend. Let's look at the calendar."

Together, Mom and Jordan went to look at the calendar on the wall by Mom's desk. "Jordan, point to the date of Matt's party. Jordan found the number 16 then pointed to the date on the calendar.

"Do you know what happens on that day?" Mom inquired.

"No. I just know it's Matt's party and I'm invited."

"Jordan, Matt's party is on a Sunday from 10:00 to 1:00. We will be at church at that time. I'm afraid you won't be able to attend after all. I'm sorry." Jordan's mom tried to hug her son who turned away.

"I don't think that's very fair," yelled a very angry Jordan.

"Why do we always have to go to church? I'm the only one in my class that goes anyway and I'll be the only one he invited that can't go to his party . . . all because of church."

Mother approached Jordan again, "Jordan, I know it doesn't sound fair, but going to church is what our family does. We aren't going to change what we do just to please others, or to be like everyone else. That wouldn't be right."

"I don't get it though. Why do we always have to go to church? I mean, we go every week and even during the week too. Can't we skip sometimes? Is it so bad not to go to church? My friends are nice, and they don't go. Why can't we be nice people too and not go to church?"

"Jordan, as Christians, we see church as a sort of celebration. Every week we are celebrating the fact that Jesus lives and that He wants us to know Him better. Think about how often you like to go to your friend's house to play. If you only went a few times a year, you wouldn't know your friend very well. When you visit their house, you are getting to know him and his family better. Going to church is like that. We go on the first day of the week, according to our calendar, because Jesus rose from the dead on the first day of the week. We go so that we can worship God in His house and get to know Him better. If we only went a few times a year, we wouldn't know God or His family very well. Everyone who belongs to God is a part of His family. We are all one family in Christ. We want to know each other and learn from each other too."

"Okay. So, why can't we just miss sometimes? God won't get mad at us will he?" Jordan asked.

"It depends on our heart. It depends on why we are missing church. If we are missing church because something "better" came up that we wanted to do, but didn't have to do, that would mean our priorities were not in line with God's. However, if something came up that demanded our attention and that we miss, like someone being sick, that wouldn't be misusing our priorities. God knows our hearts, and He knows why we do what we do. The Bible tells us that God is slow to get angry, but He can be disappointed if we make foolish decisions that don't bring honor to Him. Whether we are going to church, going to work or school, or playing with friends, we should always seek to bring honor to God."

"But doesn't God know how important this party is to me, Mom. Why should I have to choose between it and church?"

"God does know how important Matt's party is to you. He wants you to be happy, but God is much more concerned with us being obedient to Him than being happy. As your parents, we want you to enjoy church. We want your best friends to be those that go to church and share our same values. If we value something, that means we treasure and respect it. By going often to church we are showing others that we value what we learn when we are at church and the friends we have there. We are also saying that we value God's word. I know that it's hard to not be a part of something that other people are doing, like the party. Feeling left out isn't easy, but choosing to obey God is always the right way to go. Choosing between church and the party will be a witness to Matt and his family about what we value and that we are Christians who take our commitment to Christ seriously."

"Mom," Jordan began, "even though I don't like missing the party, I do like going to church, and I like my friends there. I still want to go, but I understand."

"If you'd like, I'll call his mom and explain for you so that you don't have to tell him yourself. I know that can be very difficult. We can take the present to his house on Saturday too so that you can still see him and wish him a happy birthday."

"That sounds good. Can we go shopping for the present tomorrow?"

Let's Talk About the Story

Who got invited to a birthday party?
Why couldn't he go?
Do you think that is fair or right?
What would you do if you were Jordan's mom or dad?

Prayer

Dear Father,

Thank you for giving us a church family that we can belong to. Thank you for all the fun that we have there and the good things we learn. Help us to listen when we are there and learn more and more about you every week. Amen.

Family Activity

Talk about times when you were growing up and had to miss something fun because of church. By doing so, you will be letting your kids know that you understand how they feel and don't judge them for feeling the way that they do. Then talk about fun times you've had at church, and let them tell about some of their favorite memories at church, or their favorite activities.

References: Ephesians 5: 25–26; Hebrews 10: 25

Week Four–What is Faith?

Hebrews 11:6

Without faith it is impossible to please God,* because any-one who comes to him must believe that he exists and that he rewards those who earnestly seek him. (NIV)

But without faith it is impossible to please him:* for he that cometh to God must believe that he is, and that he is a rewarder of them that diligently seek him. (KJV)

" . . . and thank you for hearing us and already answering our prayer. Amen." Grandpa finished praying then looked up from his chair at his grandson, Joseph. Everyone in the room had been praying for Joseph's grandmother who was in the hospital. She had gotten very sick a few days ago and doctors still didn't know what was wrong. They had done everything they could to help her, but she continued to lay silent, in a coma. Joseph was her youngest grandchild and didn't quite know what to make of everything that had taken place over the last few days. Joseph especially didn't know what to think about all their friends gathered at his grandpa's house, praying for his grandmother. He knew that it was good to pray for people who were sick and he knew that he wanted his grandmother to be well soon, but he wasn't quite sure how prayer worked and why everyone was praying so much for her. Didn't God hear them the first time?

"Dad, why did Granddad tell God thanks for already answering his prayer? Is Grandma coming home today? Is she all well now?"

Sadly, Dad answered, "No, Joseph, she is still very ill."

"So why'd he say it like that then? Was he trying to trick me?"

"Oh, no, Joseph, Granddad would never trick you like that. I'm sorry it seemed like a trick to you. I can see why you would feel that way though. Granddad told God 'thank you' because he believes that if we ask God for something according to what He desires, God will give it to us. That's called faith, and without faith, no one can ever please God."

"So Granddad told God thanks even before God had given him something?"

"That's right, son. It's similar to you asking me for something that you really, really want. If I felt it was a good gift that wouldn't harm you and there were no reasons not to, I would give it to you. I might even tell you that I would be going to the store later on today to pick it up and would bring it home after work. Since you know I would never lie to you, and you know that you can trust me with all your heart, you would know without a doubt that I will come home with your request. Because of this, you might go ahead and say 'thanks.' I have not yet given you the item you wanted, but you trust me enough to know that I will give it to you since you asked and it is an important request. God works in much the same way."

Eight-year-old Joseph thought for a long time before responding. "Dad, since Granddad told Him thanks, does that mean that Grandma will be coming home soon?"

"Joseph, you are asking some very important questions. I wish they were easy to answer, but they aren't. Whenever Christians begin talking about faith, it's never easy. We don't know how God works or why He works the way that He does, but we trust Him to do only what's best for us. Sometimes the way God answers may not seem best to us at the time, but later we can see how it was. If Grandma were to die and go to heaven, you probably wouldn't think it was the best thing for us; however, being in heaven in the presence of God is so wonderful that it would definitely be the best thing for Grandma. We can't pray selfishly. We have to pray for what's best for everyone, even if it hurts us for a while. When you heard Granddad pray earlier, he also prayed that God's will would be done, and he prayed that God would heal her in His time and in His way. God may choose to heal Grandma quickly and have her home with us soon. He may also choose to heal her slowly. But, Joseph, God has the right to choose to heal Grandma's body by taking her home to be with Him in heaven where she will forever be free from sickness and pain. We have to give Him the choice because He is God. We belong to God and we trust Him to do what's best for each of His children, like your grandmother. Granddad said thank you to God because he knows that God will answer his request. It may not be in the way that we would prefer, but it will always be in the right way. It's all about learning to live by faith. Living by faith means that we trust God no matter what happens. No matter how hard life gets, we trust God to provide for us, to protect us, to guide us in decisions and to meet our needs, even when we don't see the answers right away."

"Dad, you said that faith was hard to understand, but I understand it. All we have to do is follow God the way that you want me to follow you and Mom. Right? I can do that. I might not always like it, but I know I can do it. I do it everyday!"

Let's Talk About the Story

Who was in the hospital?

Why did Granddad tell God thank you before she was well?

What's one question that Joseph had for his dad?

Can you tell someone what faith is?

Prayer

Dear Father,

Thank you for teaching us how to live by faith. Help us to trust you more each day as we follow you. Help us to remember that you will never do anything that isn't best for us. Amen.

Family Activity

To help your children understand more about living by faith, play a game at night outside when it's dark or put a blindfold on them. Lead them around in the dark and have them experience what it's like to trust you fully. Next, you can stand behind them a few feet away and have them fall backwards into your arms, knowing that you are going to catch them. Explain how that is the way we are supposed to trust God too. Even though we can't see everything, He is always behind us and beside us, guiding us because He can see the things that we can't see.

References: Proverbs 3:5; Romans 5:1; 2 Corinthians 5:7; Hebrews 11:1; James 2: 26

August—Fantastic Friendships

Morgan, Michael, and Macy loved to have friends over to their house to play. Usually, their mom and dad didn't mind having friends in and out of the house, especially during the long days of summer when everyone was out of school for a few months. Morgan enjoyed playing basketball or just talking with her friends. Michael on the other hand, loved riding bikes and rollerblading when he had friends over, while their younger sister Macy enjoyed playing house, coloring or following her big sister around. On really hot days all three children would play in the pool. Whatever it was they were doing, they all agreed that it was much more fun with friends.

"Friendships are a special blessing from God," Daddy had said one day. "We have to treat our friends with love and be a good friend in return for friendships to last."

Do you have special friends that you enjoy playing with? This month as you learn your memory verses, you will be learning more about friendships and how God expects you to treat your friends. You will also learn the importance of choosing good friends that honor God rather than friends that encourage you to do what's wrong. Jesus had twelve good friends that he trusted, told secrets to, and even laughed with. He knows how important it is to have fun and to have friends to play with. He also knows how it feels to be lonely, feeling like you have no friends, or feeling left out of special events. God wants to help you as you meet friends. He wants to help you learn to get along with others and learn how to say NO to some people who might not be the best for you to be playing with.

As you listen to the stories this month, think about ways that you can learn to be a better friend, even to your own brothers or sisters.

Week One–Choosing Friends

James 4:4
"... don't you know that friendship with the world is hatred toward God?* Anyone who chooses to be a friend of the world becomes an enemy of God." (NIV)

"... know ye not that the friendship of the world is enmity with God?* whosoever therefore will be a friend of the world is the enemy of God." (KJV)

Six year old Parker had just moved into town from another state far away. He missed his friends and was very lonely as he sat on the floor near his racetrack. He felt the cold metal of the small car he held tightly in his hand, remembering how he and his best friend, Jordan, used to play cars for hours without getting bored. Now he didn't have a friend anywhere to play with.

The days passed, and slowly Parker met some boys his own age to play with after school and on week-ends. One boy, Jonathan, seemed to really want to be Parker's friend. He called him on the phone a lot, even late at night, and would occasionally come over to his house unexpectedly. Parker didn't mind too much, at least it was someone to play with. Anything was better than playing by yourself all the time, he thought. Besides, Jonathan had invited Parker over to his house this upcoming weekend. That would be really fun! He hadn't been to a friend's house to play in a long time.

Mom and Dad had other thoughts on the subject though. "Parker, have you ever met Jonathan's parents?, Mom asked one day.

"Not yet, why, Mom?" Parker didn't see why that would be important at all. "Your Daddy and I would just like to know a little about your friends before you go over to their house, that's all."

"Jonathan is real nice, Mom. There's nothing to know.

He wants to be my friend and he is the same age as me. Oh, yeah, and he also likes basketball."

"I thought you didn't like basketball, Parker. When did you start liking that?" Dad had entered the conversation all of a sudden, surprising his son.

"Well, I do now since Jonathon does. Is that all? Can I go now? I want to go play with my racetrack."

Something didn't seem right to Parker's parents, so they followed him to his room, anxious to finish the talk.

"Son, Jonathan, may seem like a good friend to you, but until we know more about him, we can't let you go over to his house and play. We know they don't attend church anywhere. That doesn't mean that they are bad people, but we want you to have friends that have the same values as we do; friends who like the same things as you and who believe in God as you do."

"If I invite him to church with us, then can I go to his house and play?"

"Inviting him to church is a wonderful idea, but that doesn't mean that he is still the best choice for you at this time." Mom carefully chose her words as she kept talking. "The Bible warns us not to make close friendships with the world. 'The world' just means those people who don't love God and His word as Christians do. When we make friends with the "world" we are told that it is as if God has become our enemy. God knows that having close friendships with the wrong kind of people could hurt us."

"How could someone like Jonathan hurt me, Mom? He wants to be my friend."

"Jonathan probably wouldn't hurt you on purpose, but the things that he is allowed to do might. You know how we are very cautious with what you watch on TV or at the theater? Some people don't mind their children doing these things. They might even use words that we would find offensive, or wrong." Dad had a point. Jonathan did say things sometimes that Parker knew were wrong. It made him feel uncomfortable.

"Parker, having friends is important, but choosing good friends is even more important. Why don't we invite the Smith's from church over for a cook-out? Their son Trey is about your age, and I hear he loves cars as much as you do," Mom suggested.

"Okay," said Parker. "But can we do it this week-end? I really want to play with my cars again real soon with a friend."

Let's Talk About the Story

Who did Parker want as a friend?
Was he a good choice for Parker? Why?
According to the Bible, what kind of friends are we to have?

Prayer

Dear Heavenly Father,
Thank you for friends. Thank you for my friend_____.
Help me to be a good friend to others, and help me to learn who isn't a good friend to play with. I love you God. Amen.

Family Activity

During the week, point out values to your children as you run across them that your family finds important (such as going to church, honesty, or watching "clean" shows). Talk about why you have chosen to establish these as important guidelines in your home and daily life.

References: Proverbs 17:17; Proverbs 18:24; 1 Corinthians 15:33; 2 Corinthians 6:14; Hebrews 10:24

Week Two—Learning to Compromise

2 Timothy 2:23–24
*Don't have anything to do with foolish and stupid arguments,
because you know they produce quarrels.* *
*And the Lord's servant must not quarrel; instead, he must be
kind to everyone, . . ." (NIV)*

*But foolish and unlearned questions avoid, knowing that they
do gender strifes.* And* the servant of the Lord must not
strive; but be gentle unto all men, . . . " (KJV)*

"It's mine!"

"No, it's mine!,"

"It is not, I found it first!"

The quarreling had begun again. Lately it seemed as if the only thing her children did was fight.

"Mom, tell her to give it back. It really is mine." Tyler's voice rang throughout the house. However, Mom had learned to ignore such trivial matters, realizing that within moments the house would be quiet down once again.

The day passed without much arguing until bedtime, at which point the noise level raised so much, earmuffs couldn't drown it out.

"Amy, you watched a show already, it's my turn."

"That was yesterday. I haven't watched anything today. So I get to pick what we watch." Amy and Tyler were fighting over who got to choose the show on television before going to bed for the evening. The argument didn't sound like it was going to be ending anytime soon, so Mom decided to help out just a bit.

"Kids, why don't you both choose a short movie, and then you can both watch what you want tonight."

"But I want to watch a long one," Amy selfishly said.

"Yeah, and I don't want to watch one of Amy's "girl" movies."

"I tell you what," said Mom, "if you two can't agree, then neither of you will be able to watch anything. You can both go to bed, and then both of you will be at fault."

That idea sure didn't sound like a great plan to either of the children. Tyler, being the oldest however, decided that he would be willing to watch one of Amy's picks if she promised he could watch one of his next. Amy likewise agreed.

As the hours passed, the children laughed the night away, eating popcorn and brownies along the way.

The next morning when Tyler and Amy began arguing again over who gets to eat the last doughnut, Mom interrupted their increasing volume with a lesson learned from the night before.

"Tyler, Amy, I was wondering, did you two have a fun time last night?"

"Yeah, it was a lot of fun, Mom. Thanks for letting us stay up so late."

"Do you think you would have had as much fun if you would have gone to bed early or spent the entire evening alone in your rooms?" Mom's questions were pretty obvious, but she wanted them to think about it.

"Kids, did you know that the Bible tells us not to argue with each other? The Bible doesn't tell us these things to make us miserable. God knows what is best for us and what will enable us to have the most fun. Arguing with each other will only lead to frustrations and anger. That can't ever be fun. God says these things are silly, or stupid."

"Mom, what if we know we are right, though?" Amy asked.

"Amy, you may think you are right, and indeed sometimes you might be right, but being right isn't what's important. Learning to get along with others through compromise is much more important. It's a lot more fun too!"

"I guess you're right, but it sure is hard not to argue, Mom," Tyler agreed.

"No it isn't, Tyler" Amy injected. "It's easy."

Well, hopefully Amy and Tyler have learned the importance of learning to get along with others, even if they don't always agree.

Let's Talk About the Story

What did Amy and Tyler first fight about?
What did mom suggest they do?
What does the Bible tell us about arguing?

Prayer

Dear God,

Sometimes it is hard to get along with others. Help me not to argue even when I think I am right. Getting along sure is more fun! I love you, God. Amen.

Family Activity

This week, emphasize getting along with others in your family time. When your children argue, send them to their rooms for immediate punishment. However, when they are working to get along, reward their efforts and compliment them. As an added twist, if they are old enough, have them catch you when you begin arguing with someone.

References: Romans 12:16; Romans 14:19; Romans 15:5; Timothy 2:14,16; Titus 3:9; 2

Week Three—Do Unto Others As . . .

Matthew 7:12

So in everything, do to others what you would have them do to you,* for this sums up the Law and the Prophets. (NIV)

Therefore all things whatsoever ye would that men should do to you, do ye even so to them:* for this is the law and the prophets. (KJV)

Five-year-old Ashley ran to her mommy's arms with tears streaming down her face. "Honey, what's the matter? Did you get hurt?" Mom asked, holding her daughter close.

"No, Brittany just called me a name and then drew on the picture I was making for you."

"I'm sorry, Ashley. Why do you think she did a thing like that?"

"I don't know, Mommy, but I'm gonna go back and draw on her picture too. She shouldn't have done that to me." Ashley was very angry at her three-year-old cousin, Brittany. She couldn't wait to get back at her for what she had done.

But Mom had other plans for Ashley, plans that didn't involve hurting her cousin. "Ashley, you have a right to be angry at Brittany right now. She shouldn't have done that to you, but getting back at her like that isn't the best way to handle your anger."

"Why not, Mommy? She was mean to me, so I'm going to be mean back!"

"Ashley, do you remember when Mrs. Herndon from church wasn't acting very kind to some of us?"

"Yes, ma'am. She was being mean too."

"What she did hurt us, but we decided to pray for her and try to find a way that we might be able to help her rather than be mean to her."

"Why did you do that? She didn't deserve it."

"Maybe not, but the Bible teaches us as Christians to treat others according to how we *want* to be treated, not by what they have done to us. It's called the "Golden Rule". I like to think of it as being the most valuable rule, or lesson, for us to follow. Just like real gold costs a lot of money and is very valuable, this "rule" that Jesus gave to us is also priceless, like gold, when it comes to getting along with others. Sometimes it is hard to treat others the way we want to be treated instead of treating them the way they deserve."

"Did Mrs. Herndon start being nice again?" Ashley was very interested in what Mom had to say all of a sudden.

"As a matter of fact, yes, she did. And she felt very bad for the way she had acted. She asked us to forgive her and we did." Mom brushed Ashley's hair away from her face as she wiped the tears from her eyes. Ashley was beginning to smile once again.

"Are y'all still friends?" Ashley asked curiously.

"Mrs. Herndon is a very good friend of mine. We're even planning on getting together tomorrow for lunch."

"Mama, if I'm nice to Brittany, will she be nice to me again?"

"Oh, I think you can count on that. Sometimes people just have bad days. They don't really mean to hurt others; it's just the way things happen. If you react to Brittany by hurting her like she did you, it may take much longer to be friends again. The best thing to do is to do something nice, just as if she never hurt you. You might want to tell her that what she did made you mad, but God would still want you to treat her the way you want to be treated . . . and don't you always want to be treated nicely?"

"Okay Mommy, I won't draw on her picture, but can we play with the play dough now?" Ashley seemed to have learned a good lesson about treating others the way she would want to be treated. Best of all, the two cousins spent the rest of the day playing and sharing the way God would want them too.

Let's Talk About the Story

Why was Ashley mad at her cousin?
Did Brittany deserve for Ashley to treat her nice?
What did Mom tell Ashley to do?
Have you ever gotten mad at a friend and wanted to get back at them? What does the Bible teach us about how to treat others?

Prayer

Dear God,
Sometimes when people are mean, I want to be mean back. It doesn't seem very fair. Help me to treat them the way you want me to, *and* the way that I want to be treated. Thank you for friends. I love you God. Amen.

Family Activity

Before an incident occurs, talk to your kids about positive ways they can treat others who might insult them or hurt them. Pray for anyone that might be offending your child already and pray for your child's reactions to that person. Help them to understand that we don't treat others according to how they treat us, but how we want to be treated.

References: Matthew 5:44; Matthew 22:39; John 13:34; Romans 12:17–18; Romans 14:13, 19; Romans 15:1–2, 7

Week Four—Strength When Tempted

2 Chronicles 19:11
Be fearless in your stand for truth and honesty. And may
God use you to defend the innocent. (Living Bible)*

James 4:7–8a
*Submit yourselves, then to God. Resist the devil, and he will
flee from you.* Come near to God and
he will come near to you. (NIV)*

*Submit yourselves therefore to God. Resist the devil, and he
will flee from you.* Draw nigh to God, and he will draw nigh
to you. (KJV)*

12 year old Garrett was enjoying the hot summer day, riding bikes and playing with his friends in the neighborhood. He was looking forward to riding to the park where the three boys were going to play soccer in the grassy field. On the way, Garrett saw 11 year old Travis, his new neighbor, sitting on the grass with his bike laying beside him. A ball and glove lay nearby. As he got closer, Garrett could tell that Travis was crying, though trying very hard to hide the tears from the older boys who were around. Travis hadn't lived in the neighborhood long. His family had moved just a few months ago from another state. Garrett didn't know him well. Garrett's mother had explained to him that Travis had some differences that made it harder for him to do certain things. She said that Travis had something called Autism and because of that he had a harder time making friends, playing sports and understanding some things that many kids his own age might find very easy to understand. Garrett hadn't thought much about it until now. Travis looked like all his other friends. He didn't look different. He had never tried to make friends with Travis; he figured Travis could find his own friends just like Garrett had. But today seemed different. He had stopped

to see if Travis was alright or if he needed any help. Slowly Travis told him that he had fallen off his bike while trying to ride to the park to play ball.

"Did you hurt yourself?" a concerned Garrett asked.

"Just a little. I hurt my knee, but I'll be okay."

Garrett saw his friends waiting off to the side, making eyes at him, and motioning for him to hurry up so that they could get to the soccer field before other kids were there. Garrett had been looking forward to playing soccer all day with them, but he couldn't leave Travis there all alone, knowing he didn't have anyone to play with. Finally he said, "Travis, how 'bout if you and I go to the park together and play catch for a while."

"I don't know. I can't catch or throw very well. You'll be a lot better than me."

"That's okay" said Garrett. I had to learn once too. I don't mind helping you if you don't mind." Travis smiled and stood up.

The other boys couldn't believe what they had heard. Was Garrett really dumping them to play with Travis? Garrett went over to explain, but it didn't seem that his friends really wanted to understand. They were in a hurry to leave. He could tell they were angry at him. Their actions and words hurt, but Garrett felt good about his decision. As they rode their bikes to the park together, Garrett knew that he had made the right choice. He would have other opportunities to play with his friends. Travis needed a friend too. And frankly, Garrett realized he could always use one more friend. At the end of the day when he was going to bed, he thought about the day. He told his mom all about it. He hadn't done what he had planned, but he had had a great day anyway. "Travis may be different from me in some ways", he said, "but we're a lot alike too. He's really nice and he likes to read the same kind of books that I do.

"I'm glad you were his friend today, Garrett", said his mom. "You did a good thing by helping someone who needed a friend. I know it was hard to leave your friends and change your plans. I'm sure you were really tempted to go on to the soccer field with them, but by resisting the temptation to do that and help someone in need, you ended up with a new friend.

"I know Mom. Isn't that cool? It was very hard to say no to my friends, but I knew Travis was upset and I really didn't want to leave him there alone. I know things are harder for him, but I really like him. It doesn't matter to me that he is autistic. I'm glad I got to know him today. I hope he wants to play with me tomorrow too." With that, Garrett's mom kissed him good night. She was proud of her son. She knew that with God's help, Garrett would be able to make many wise decisions as He grew and would be able to resist the temptations that were a part of life.

Let's Talk About the Story

What was Garrett wanting to do for the day?

What changed his mind?

Did He make a good decision, even though his friends were mad at him?

Can you think of a time when you were tempted to do something? What did you do?

Prayer

Dear Father,

Thank you for giving us friends of all kinds. Help us to resist temptation and make good decisions, even when others might not understand. Helps us to be friends to others', even when they are different from us. Amen.

Family Activity

As you discuss the verse this week, remind them of the importance of resisting the temptation to do what might be easier, in order to do what is nobler. Talk about a time with them when you were tempted to do something and what you did. Did you make a good decision? How did you feel about your decision afterwards? Talk about how hard it can sometimes be to make decisions that aren't always the most popular. Remind them that no matter what we are tempted to do, God will always be near us to help in our time of need. Whether it be in obeying basic family rules, or situations on TV shows, use this time to reinforce how to be strong when faced with temptation. Role play ways to practice saying no in various circumstances.

References: Acts 5:29; 1 Corinthians 15:58; 1 Corinthians 10:12–14; 2 Timothy 2:19; Hebrews 2:18; 1 John 4:4

September—Building Strong Values

During this month of devotions, you will be learning about the word "values," what it means, and what they are. Everyone *has* values, but *following* our values is sometimes harder than owning them. The word *"value"* means something that you cherish or think highly of. You can value your dolls, your special blanket, your quarter collection, your high grades in school, your family, or your friends. There are many things that people value. Taking pride in something and finding value in it is not a sin. We should all have values and work towards keeping them, but sometimes it's hard to keep some things that we value, especially if those with whom we play don't find value in the same things. That's when we might be tempted to give up our value system and adopt the values of other people, even if we really don't agree with it. Valuing a toy is much easier than valuing a friendship with someone that many people don't like. It would be much easier to stop being friends with someone than to keep the friendship when other people laugh at us. No one likes to be made fun of because it can hurt.

According to God's Word, the Bible, we should aim at having strong character values. Values such as working hard, being a good friend, being honest, and being responsible are character values. That means they are things that we treasure but they aren't toys we can play with or hold. They are goals or ideas that we hold close in our hearts that determine how we live our lives. Everyone values something and no one's values are exactly like anyone else's, although many of them may be the same. As you read through this month's stories, see if you can decide what some of your values are. What do you hold dear to your heart? Do you value time with your mom? Do you value story time every night with Dad? Do you value lots of fun time with your friends?

Let's Talk About Values

What are values?
Who has values?
Are values bad to have?
Name some values that some people may have.

Week One–Always Do Your Best

Colossians 3:23
Whatever you do, work at it with all your heart, as working for the Lord, not for men. (NIV)

And whatsoever ye do, do it heartily, as to the Lord, and not unto men. (KJV)

It was the first Saturday of the month and that meant only one thing to Eric. He knew he was going to have to spend the day helping his dad around the house, doing whatever needed to be done. Today he wanted to play baseball with his friends at the ball park then go to the movies. He knew better than to ask though, he had tried that too many times before.

By 9:00 A.M. Eric and his dad had already started on the yard. First it was moving, then edging, then raking. After that they had to lay some cedar chips in Mom's garden. It wasn't that yard work was so terrible, Eric thought, but he'd rather be playing with his friends today. If the weather was good enough for yard work, wasn't it even better for playing baseball? After lunch Eric' dad told him to clean out the storage shed while he fertilized the yard. That was probably the worst job Eric could think of doing. He'd rather clean garbage cans than to clean out the shed. All the dust, the junk, the spider webs, and the many boxes of unknown items were too much for him. He did the work, but he was not happy about it. And he was going to let his father know how he felt every chance he got.

By 3:00 most of the work had been done. Or so he thought.

"Dad, are we through yet? I'm sick of doing all this work. I have better things to do with my time on a Saturday than to feel like a slave, you know."

"I'm sorry you feel that way Eric because I've just come up with another two things you can do by yourself. I think I'll go in and rest a while." Dad gave him the next set of instructions, patted Eric on the back and went inside the air conditioned house."

By now Eric was more than angry. Why should I have to work when Dad isn't even willing to work, he thought to himself. After a few minutes of thinking about it, he finally decided that he was going inside and tell his dad how he felt. "Dad, I want to know why you think it's okay for me to do all this work while you're in here resting?" Eric asked indignantly.

"I'm glad you asked Eric. Why don't you sit down while I explain to you what's on my mind." Eric could tell his dad was being somewhat sarcastic. "The truth is that until you spoke to me the way you did about having to do so much work, I was about to call it a day for both of us and give you some money for the movies with your friends. However, after the attitude that came out of your mouth, I decided that a little more work wouldn't hurt you. I am in here resting because after a full day of work, I'm tired. I'm sure you are too, but the difference is that I didn't speak to you with disrespect the way you spoke to me. I was disappointed in your attitude because I thought that after all these years of working together, you had learned a lesson about good work ethics. You see Eric, even though I didn't mention it to you, I'm not feeling well today. I have a tremendous headache, but I knew that the work needed to get done so I did it without complaining. I knew that I could rest after the work was completed, and I'd rest better knowing it was behind me."

"But Dad, why do I have to help all the time? None of my other friends have to do this much work on weekends. Besides, I go to school every day and do homework. Don't I deserve a break?"

Dad responded, "Eric, we all work hard around here doing what we need to do. The weekends are the only time we have to do some of the work that can't get done during the week because we are at work and school. Your mother and I value hard work. The Bible teaches us that whatever we do, we are to do it as if we are working for the Lord. I don't always like what my boss wants me to do at the office, but in those situations, I pretend that God is my boss and I am working for him. That always seems to help my attitude. A bad attitude never earned anyone a promotion or respect at work. We are instructed in scripture to do our best regardless of what it may cost us. If we have worked our best, we will never have any reason to be ashamed. If you can learn to be a hard worker now and have strong, positive work ethics, whether you like the assignment or not, you will always do well. That's what I am trying to teach you."

"I'm sorry Dad. I didn't know you were feeling bad today. You worked just as hard as you always do without ever complaining about any of it. I shouldn't have talked like I did. I appreciate the way you and Mom work so hard at everything you do. I hope I can grow up to be just like that when I'm an adult. Do you think I'll ever learn how to work without complaining?" Eric asked humbly.

"I'm betting on it, son. And you can get some good practice in by finishing up those last two chores I gave you." With that, Eric' dad hugged him, and then poured him a glass of cold water as Eric headed outside one last time.

Let's Talk About the Story

What did Eric have to help his dad do?
Did he want to?
What was Eric wanting to do?

What important lesson did he learn from a day of hard work?

Prayer

Dear Father,

Thank you for working so hard for us without resting. Help us to value hard work and never give anyone a reason to be ashamed of the work that we do. May we always glorify you in our work. Amen.

Family Activity

Take time this week to find some much needed chores that you can do as a family. Whether it's cleaning your house or going to a shut-in's house to help, work as a unit and discuss the joy that hard work brings to people. Talk about how good work ethics are pleasing to the Lord, and no matter how menial or big the task is, it's never unimportant to God.

References: Proverbs 6:10–11; Proverbs 10:4; Proverbs 16; 3; 1 Thessalonians 4:11–12; 1 Thessalonians 5:12; 2 Timothy 2:15; Hebrews 10:34–35

Week Two—Being Responsible

Galatians 6:4–5

Each one should test his own actions.* Then he can take pride in himself, without comparing himself to somebody else, for each one should carry his own load. (NIV)

But let every man prove his own work,* and then shall he have rejoicing in himself alone, and not in another. For every man shall bear his own burden. (KJV)

Learning to be responsible can be a hard lesson to learn. Sometimes we don't want to be responsible. Many times we don't want to be responsible because it involves more work and we want to play. But sometimes we don't want to be responsible because it means having to be honest and take the blame for mistakes that we make. We might even get punished for those mistakes. If we know we will be punished, who would want to admit to doing something wrong? Lying or even not saying anything at all would be easier sometimes. But God has a different plan for us. He wants us to be responsible and take responsibility for our actions even if it means it will cost us something.

Carley wanted to wear her sister's new sweater to the mall with her friends. Her sister had already told her not to last week when she asked. Carley loved the sweater though, and she knew her friends would think it was cool. She borrowed the sweater anyway and promised herself she would take good care of it. Her sister wouldn't even miss it. While she was eating at the mall, she accidentally spilled some ice cream on it. It left a spot. She knew her mom would be able to get it out, but not if she didn't know. Now, Carley would have to tell her mom and her sister that she wore the sweater to the mall. Her friends tried to tell her not to tell and instead act like her sister got it on there when she wore it last. Being responsible means that Carley would have to tell what really happened, even though her sister would probably get upset and her mom would probably punish her.

Abigail was very tired. It seemed too early to be getting out of bed, so she didn't get up when her dad called her . . . the first time, or the second time. The bed felt too good and she was too sleepy. She was running late the rest of the morning since she didn't get out of bed on time. Abigail was in such a hurry to get out the door that she forgot her tennis shoes that she needed to wear for playing basketball after school. This wasn't the first time that she had forgotten something. Last week her mom brought her lunch to her, then earlier this week she had forgotten her homework. Her mom had told her she wasn't going to be bringing anything else to her that she had forgotten. Abigail called her mom as soon as she remembered about her tennis shoes. What should her mom do? Abigail needs to learn about being responsible. While the shoes are very important if she wants to play ball, learning to be responsible is even more important. Abigail's mom was right to tell her that she wouldn't be making anymore trips to the school for her daughter. If she never forces her daughter to take care of her own belongings, she will never see the need to be responsible.

Both Carley and Abigail had some hard lessons to learn. They needed to be responsible for something that they did. Sometimes being responsible isn't easy. Sometimes it's very hard. God tells us to be responsible for our own actions and not to blame others when we are the ones who forget something, or make a mistake. When you blame someone else for your mistakes, you are cheating yourself out of growing up. If you do it enough times, others will begin to not trust you. No one likes getting blamed for something they didn't do. Everyone makes mistakes. Your parents, teachers, the preacher at your church, and even your grandparents make mistakes. But those who value honesty and responsibility have learned that it's easier to accept responsibility up front than it is to live with a lie and always blame others.

Let's Talk About the Story

What did Carley want to do?

Did she make a good choice?

What should she do when she gets home?

What do you think will happen?

Why did Abigail forget her tennis shoes?

Was she being responsible at her house before she left for school?

What should her mom do to help her daughter be more responsible?

Have you ever forgotten to do something and wanted someone else to help you out?

How are some ways that you are not responsible?

What are things that you do that are responsible?

How can your parents help you learn to be more responsible?

What does God want us to do?

Prayer

Dear Father,

Thank you for forgiving us when we are not responsible. When we forget to do things or blame others for our own actions, remind us what you desire. Help us to remember that being responsible is a part of growing up. Amen.

Family Activity

Talk about ways that people show responsibility. If you are walking your dog and keep him on a leash, that is being responsible. If you throw your trash away, you are being responsible. If you see someone turning in a lost item, they are being responsible. Explain to your children how being irresponsible can cause them to make bad grades, not get a good job, or even get fired from a job. Being irresponsible always leads to negative outcomes while being responsible leads to life and success.

References: Matthew 12:37; 1 Corinthians 7:24; Hebrews 4:13

Week Three–Honesty is the Best Policy

Psalms 34:13–14

Keep your tongue from evil and your lips from speaking lies. Turn from evil and do good; seek peace and pursue it. (NIV)

Keep thy tongue from evil, and they lips from speaking guile. Depart from evil, and do good; seek peace, and pursue it. (KJV)

"Justin, where did you get this candy?" Candy had fallen out of Justin's jacket pocket as Mom was picking up in the living room. She knew she had not given him any that day, nor had she given him any money.

"Oh, that, well, uh, I got it from Jacob; he didn't want it." Nine-year-old Justin had to think fast where that candy came from. He knew he would be in big trouble if he told his mom the *truth*.

"When were you with Jacob today? I thought he was supposed to be out of town."

Uh, oh. Now he was in a mess. Justin had forgotten that it was spring break and that his best friend Jacob was going out of town for a few days. Now what was he going to do? He certainly didn't want to get in trouble.

"No, they changed their mind. I saw him this morning when I went bike riding."

"That's very interesting, Justin. When I drove by their house earlier today, I saw them loading up the van and heading out. Are you sure there's not more you need to tell me?"

With that, as grown up as he felt, Justin began to cry. He knew he had told a lie to cover for stealing the candy from the local corner store. He decided to tell his mom everything, even if he did get in a lot of trouble.

After he had confessed, he felt better, but his Mom had

a few things to say to him, and he knew his punishment was coming.

"Justin, when we are tempted to do wrong, we have a choice to make. We can either do what is wrong, or we can do the right thing. Sometimes doing the right thing seems harder than choosing to do what is wrong. When we feel trapped by our choices to do right or wrong, that is called 'temptation.' Temptation isn't bad; it is just part of life. But, we are still responsible for the choices we make. Lying and stealing are like that. When you feel you really want to steal something, you probably feel trapped, or tempted. You know it is wrong, yet you still really want it. The Bible tells us that it is the devil who is putting those thoughts in our head to do what is wrong, but if we resist him, he will leave you alone."

"Mom, how do you resist the devil? That sounds hard." Justin was listening carefully to all his mom had to say.

"We can resist the devil by asking God for help. God wants us to do what is right, and He is always ready to help us. Son, God knows how hard it is to always do what is right and to tell the truth all the time. He knows you will make mistakes as you grow. Mom and Daddy still make mistakes too, but if you learn to ask God for help when you are tempted to do what is wrong, He WILL help you." Mom looked deep into her son's eyes as she gently spoke from her heart.

"Justin, you have to learn that whenever anybody asks or tells you to do something that you know is not right, you have to find the strength inside of you to say no to them, even if they laugh at you for it. When you make bad choices, you are the only one responsible for it. It's up to you to do what is right."

"Mom, I'm sorry I lied to you, and I'm sorry I stole the candy. Will you forgive me? I really want to do what is right. It doesn't feel very good to have to hide things from you."

"Of course I will forgive you. I love you *so* much. Now, let's talk about taking this candy back to the store and talking to the manager."

Let's Talk About the Story

What did Justin do that was wrong?

How did he feel about his actions?

What does the Bible tell us about speaking the truth?

How can we find the strength to do what is right when we feel tempted to do what is wrong?

Prayer

Dear God,

Sometimes it sure is tempting to do the wrong thing. Help me to make good choices, like telling the truth, even when friends want me to do what I know is wrong. Thank you for always helping us everyday. I love you, God. Amen.

Family Activity

Tell about a time when you told a lie and how you felt afterwards. Children need to know that we are not perfect and that we make mistakes even as adults. Give examples of what would happen if everyone in the family lied to each other. What would happen to the trust we have? Remind them that God loves us and forgives everyone for their sins, no matter what, when we ask with a sincere heart.

References: Exodus 20:16; Proverbs 6:16–19; Proverbs 12:17–19, 22; John 8:43–44; Colossians 3:8–10; Titus 1:2; Hebrews 6:18

Week Four- True to Yourself

1 Corinthians 15:58
Therefore, my dear brothers, stand firm. Let nothing move you.* Always give yourselves fully to the work of the Lord, because you know that your labor in the Lord is not in vain.
(NIV)
Therefore, my beloved brethren, be ye stedfast, unmoveable,* always abounding in the work of the Lord, forasmuch as ye know that your labour is not in vain in the Lord. (KJV)

Polly and Samantha had been best friends for years. Their parents were also friends. They liked the same things and enjoyed spending as much time together as they could. As they got older, Polly began to change. She had new friends at school that Samantha didn't have. She started doing things and going places that she had never done before. What's worse, these were the very things they said they would never do. Samantha was very sad. She didn't want to tell her parents why she wasn't spending as much time with her best friend as she used to. She still really liked Polly and didn't want her to get in trouble. So, Samantha spent her weekends in her room or with her brother, Stuart. It wasn't as much fun as playing with Polly, but at least she wasn't always alone.

One day while Samantha was walking her dog at the park, she ran into Polly. Polly was taking care of her little brother Peter. She was pushing Peter on the swing when Samantha appeared. Inside, Samantha was scared to see her friend, yet she also felt a little excited too. She remembered all the fun times they used to have at the park together until the last three months. "Hi, Polly," Samantha said first.

"Hi Samantha, what are you doing here?"

As the conversation continued, they slowly began to laugh together. Samantha was excited thinking that she and Polly were getting back together again. Soon however, Heather and Lilly appeared. They were some of Polly's new friends. It wasn't long before Polly changed her attitude towards Samantha and began acting like she didn't even know her, or like her. As the girls started talking, Samantha heard them planning another party at a friend's house where they were going to do things that Samantha didn't want to participate in. She knew it was wrong. Both girls' parents had raised them to know right from wrong and to know how to make wise choices, even when it was hard. Maybe that's why it was so hard for Samantha to see her best friend like this. They both knew it was wrong. Heather looked at Samantha and asked if she would like to come to the party. Samantha wanted to have fun again with Polly. She wanted to do something with girls her own age. She had felt rejected and left out by Polly and her new friends, but now that she had an invitation, she knew it would be wrong to accept it. Or would it?

Standing up for what's right is often very hard to do. Knowing right from wrong is the easy part. Doing it is the harder part. But as Christians, we are called by God to make the tough choices and do what's right even when others don't. Being popular or having lots of friends is fun. It's okay to have many friends and do fun things with them as long as they have the same values as you do and follow the same rules. When friends start tempting you to do what is wrong they are no longer good friends. True friends will always respect your values and not make fun of others for believing differently. Standing up for what is right is hard, especially when it means you might loose a friend because of it. But when you choose to be true to yourself, no matter what the cost, you will always be the winner.

Let's Talk About the Story

Who were Polly and Samantha?

What was the problem in the story?

Did Polly know right from wrong? Did Samantha?

Why do you think Polly started doing things that her parents wouldn't approve of?

What should Samantha do? Should she go to the party so that she and Polly can be friends again, or should she turn down the invitation?

Prayer

Dear Father,

Thank you for teaching us how to stand up for what is right. It's hard to be the only one to do the right thing. Feeling lonely and different never feels good. You too were all alone so we know you understand. Help us to make wise choices with friends and in our activities even when no one else seems to care. Amen.

Family Activity

To encourage your children to stand up for what is right when others don't, play a game with them one evening. Do role plays offering them to do things that aren't good (choose age appropriate activities), and have each child practice saying no. Put extra pressure on them to say yes, but not so much that they end up in tears. Have each child take turns playing both sides. Afterwards, talk about how it made them feel and what they learned from the exercise. Remind them that even when choices are hard, God is always present to give them the strength to say no.

References: Romans 1:16; 1 Corinthians 16:13; 2 Timothy 1:12

October—Those Crazy Feelings!

Feelings! Feelings! Wonderful feelings.
Everyone has them no matter who you are.
Feelings can feel good, and some feel kind of sad.
God created feelings and none of them are bad.

Whether it's being happy, sad, angry, or silly, everyone has feelings! Best of all, all feelings are okay. This month the Bible lessons are going to be talking about different feelings that we may have and how to handle them in appropriate ways. Since God made all of our feelings as a way to express how we feel on the inside, and since God never makes mistakes, we know that all feelings are normal. The way you feel is . . . well, it's the way you feel and that's all. Sometimes people may think that some feelings are wrong to have while other feelings are good. The truth is that feelings are "neutral." That means they are neither bad nor good. Feelings are like a thermometer that your mom or dad uses to see if you have a fever. A thermometer is just an instrument to let others know that you are sick. Feelings are a thermometer that let you and others know how you feel about things. While it is true that feelings are neither bad nor good, what we do with our feelings can be wrong. If you are angry and call your brother names, that would be wrong. Being angry isn't what is wrong, but calling someone names is the part that makes it not okay. This may sound confusing right now, but by the time you finish reading all of the stories this month, you will understand feelings much better. Just remember this, feelings are God's gift to us, but we need to learn how to use our feelings in healthy ways that don't hurt us, or other people.

Let's Talk About Feelings

Can you name some feelings you have had today?

Are feelings bad?
Who gave us feelings?

Week One–I've Got the Joy, Joy, Joy, Joy!!

Proverbs 15:13
A happy heart makes the face cheerful, but heartache crushes the spirit. (NIV)

A merry heart maketh a cheerful countenance: but by sorrow of the heart the spirit is broken. (KJV)

The Robinson's were all gathered for their yearly family reunion. Everyone always looked forward to this time of year because they had such a good time laughing, playing together and eating good food. Each evening before going to bed, all the families gathered in the living room for a time of singing around the piano, a short Bible thought, and prayer.

"Besides all the laughing, the singing is the best part of the whole day," whispered six-year old Noelle to her mom as she was being tucked in bed.

Her mom leaned down and hugged her daughter, then kissed her forehead. "I like the singing too, but tell me why it is that you like it so much," said her mom.

"Well, it's like I get this good feeling inside my heart whenever we sing, even if I don't know the song. I like to sing, but I also like to listen to the grownups singing when I don't know the words. It kind of feels happy to me, just like when I laugh with Austyn and Erin and Cassandra. What's that called, Mom, when you feel that kind of good?"

Her mom smiled at her then answered, "I think the feeling you are talking about is what the Bible calls JOY. Joy is more than feeling happy and laughing. Joy goes much deeper than giggles. It is a comfortable, warm feeling, even when nothing funny is happening, but you don't know why."

"Yeah, I think that's it. That sounds like the way the music makes me feel when we're all together singing and Grandpa is playing the piano for us."

"Music makes us all feel better, I think. Being happy is a wonderful feeling. Everyone likes to feel happy. Laughter is also a wonderful way to express your happiness. Did you know that God talks a lot about laughing and being happy in the Bible?"

"No way! Does God like to laugh too then," asked a surprised Noelle?

"I wouldn't be surprised. He speaks of it plenty of times. We are told that laughter is the best medicine for us, that a happy heart makes us cheerful, and that there is a time to laugh and dance. Not only does God talk about laughing, He even mentions music and singing several times in His Word too."

"God sure must want us to be happy since He mentions it so much. I didn't know that He cared that much about us being happy. I thought He just wanted us to obey Him and follow lots of rules, that's all." As Noelle reached up high for a last big stretch, her mom couldn't resist one big "goodnight tickle" for sweet dreams. Noelle squealed with delight as her mom tickled her some more.

After she settled down a bit, she tucked her little girl in tight, and fluffed up the pillow for good measure. As Noelle pulled the blanket closer to her neck and buried her head down in the pillow, she could hear her grandfather still playing softly at the piano. She drifted off to sleep, still hearing his voice singing, "I've got peace, love and joy like a river, I've got peace, love, and joy like a river, I've got peace, love, and joy like a river in my soul. . . ." That night as Noelle went to sleep, she finally knew what it meant to have joy like a river. And she had to agree, she did have joy, just like a bubbling river, in her heart tonight.

Let's Talk About the Story

Why was all of Noelle's family together?
Did they like being together, or did it make them mad?
How did Noelle say that the music made her feel?
What is JOY?

Prayer

Dear Father,

Thank you so much for the gift of joy. It feels so good to share joy with others. Thank you for all the nice things that bring us joy, like music, families, and warm blankets.

Help us to share your joy with others, especially when they are feeling sad. Amen.

Family Activity

Ask your family what some of their favorite "free" activities are to do as a family. Then, when they aren't expecting it, plan to initiate some of those ideas. Later, talk about how those activities made each of them feel. Discuss the difference between joy and sadness, and joy and happiness. You might explain that everyday when you wake up and see them smile, that brings you joy, but when they do well on a test, say something funny, or score points in basketball, that makes you happy.

References: Ecclesiastes 3:1, 4; Psalm 28: 7; Proverbs 17:22; Psalm 126; Isaiah 55: 12; John 10:10; Philippians 4:1; 1 Thessalonians 5:16

Week Two—No S'more Tears

Psalm 34:18
The Lord is close to the brokenhearted and saves those who are crushed in spirit. (NIV)

The Lord is nigh unto them that are of a broken heart; and saveth such as be of a contrite spirit. (KJV)

Daniel was sad. Very sad. His cat "S'mores" had died that morning and he missed her terribly. He didn't feel like doing anything except sitting on his bed and thinking about how nice S'mores had always made him feel. He had been a good cat. Daniel had him ever since he could remember. All six years of his life, and that was a very long time for a little boy. He loved his fish and liked his canary, but his cat was extra special. He didn't think he would ever feel happy again. He wasn't even sure he wanted to. He lay his head down on his pillow and started to cry when his big brother, Mark walked in. Mark was much older than he was and always knew how to make Daniel feel better. Mark sat down on the bed beside Daniel and patted his back. He didn't say anything. Together they sat in the silence for what seemed forever when Daniel finally turned over to look at his big brother.

"Hey there," said Mark.

"Hi," said a teary-eyed Daniel. What were you doing in here all this time?"

"Just sitting and being with you. I didn't know what to say, so I thought it might be better if I just sat and didn't say anything. Just to let you know I was here for you. That's all I know to do."

"Thanks," smiled a quiet Daniel. After a few minutes, Daniel asked his brother a question. "Mark, will I always miss S'mores? Cause I don't like feeling this way. I don't want to feel this way forever. Will the hurt ever go away?"

Mark thought for a minute then answered. "Daniel, I don't know how long you will hurt. It might be a few days, or it might be longer than that. When I was ten our dog died, and I was sad for a long time. Everyone is different. No matter how long you are sad though, you won't be sad forever. It may feel that way at the time, but it eventually gets better and then the sad just goes away for good. I still wish I had my dog, Snickers, but I don't feel sad about it anymore. Does that make sense?"

"I guess so . . . but not really. I want S'mores back with me. I want to pet him again and let him sleep with me on my pillow like he did every night. It doesn't seem fair. He was a good cat. Why did he have to die?" Tears started flowing again, so Mark held his little brother in his lap and let him cry.

"Daniel, I know that you're sad right now and nothing is going to make it feel better today. Sometimes we have to just let the sad come and not try to stop it. But I want to let you know something else. I want you to know that God sees how sad you are and He cares. His heart is breaking too. He is sad whenever we are sad. He wants to make us feel better, just like Dad wants to help you feel better, and Mom, and me. God isn't scared away by our feelings. He made them and knows how we feel. He wants us to express our feelings in good ways, like crying, and talking about how we feel. He isn't going to leave you when you are sad. He's going to stay right by your side as you sleep and as you think of all the nice thoughts you have of S'mores. Those good memories of your cat are God's way of making you feel better too. He comforts us in lots of cool ways. I don't really know how to make you feel better, Daniel. I don't know the right thing to say either, but God knows exactly what to do and what to say. He's always there for you. If you wake up in the night and miss S'mores being with you, you can tell God all about it and He'll hear you. You won't see him the way you see me here right now, but He'll be with you anyway."

"Mark," Daniel began, "I miss S'mores, but I'm glad I have you and Mom and Dad still. I'm also glad that I have God."

Daniel crawled out of his brother's lap and lay on his bed. It was almost bed time and he had had a long day.

Mark messed up his brother's hair in a way that said, "I love you," then said, "Daniel, if you'd like, I can stay with you until you fall asleep."

"That would be good. I'd like that." Mark turned the light off then sat next to his brother who was already peacefully resting.

Let's Talk About the Story

Who were Daniel and Mark?

What had happened to Daniel earlier in the day?

What did his brother tell him God does when we are sad?

Do you think God cares when you are sad?

Prayer

Dear Father,

Thank you for comforting me and caring when I am sad. Thank you for giving us people who can help us when we are sad. Help us to comfort others, just like you comfort us. Amen.

Family Activity

Tell about a time when you were sad and someone helped by comforting you. It could be when someone died, you lost a part in the school play, or you didn't get an important job offer. Tell what that person did that made you feel loved. Talk about how you have felt God's comfort during these times. Make it a family project to help someone else who needs comforting by baking cookies, visiting, making a homemade card, or cutting their grass. Let them know that God loves them.

References: Psalm 34:15; Isaiah 61:1–2; Luke 6:21b; Hebrews 12:3

Week Three—Angry Words, Hurtful Heart

Psalm 4:4
In your anger do not sin; when you are on your beds, search your hearts and be silent. (NIV)

Stand in awe, and sin not: commune with your own heart upon your bed, and be still. (KJV)

Kyle and Katy were having fun splashing in the pool. It was a hot June day and the water felt cool on their backs, faces, and feet as they jumped and swam and splashed for hours.

This is the best day ever, thought Kyle as he dove under water looking for the penny his sister had thrown in. Seconds later he zoomed to the surface, penny in hand, as he announced himself the big winner.

"That's not fair," shouted Katy from the side of the pool. "I wasn't ready. I didn't even say 'go'!" And with that, she jumped out of the pool and ran to the grass where their things were laying next to their mom. Without thinking, she took his towel and threw it in the puddle on the walkway then took his goggles and threw them at him in the pool. Mother returned from the snack stand just in time to hear Katy yelling at her brother and calling him names. Five-year-old Kyle started crying as his goggles floated out to the middle of the pool, further out than he or his sister were allowed to swim.

"Katy Tucker, what are you doing?" cried Mom. "You know better than to do such things."

Seven-year-old Katy ignored her mom and walked back to the lawn chair where she covered up in her towel. She had a hateful look on her face that told her mom she was quite angry. Disregarding her daughter, Mom went to the pool to check on Kyle who was still crying. She lifted him out of the pool and

placed a towel around his wet body, trying to console her son through the tears.

Moments later a lifeguard approached. He had recovered the goggles from the pool and was returning them to their owner. "Thank you," responded Kyle, who was beginning to calm down from the incident. Mom sat Kyle down on the grass to warm up while she took care of another matter—talking to Katy.

"Katy, you may not want to talk right now, but I need you to tell me why you got so angry at your brother. What did he do to cause you to react like that?" After Katy finished telling what happened, her mother looked at her and said, "Katy, you were very angry weren't you?" Katy nodded her head. "Your brother didn't intend to hurt you. What you did was far more serious than what he did. While he may have made you angry, only you control how you react. Kyle didn't make you call him names or throw his towel in the water. You chose to do that when you let your feelings control you rather than you controlling them. Part of being responsible means managing the way you react to people and tough situations. Things are going to make you angry in life, but you don't need to hit, throw, yell, or call people names when you are mad. When you hurt others or their belongings, or even damage your own property, it is a sin. As Christians we want to please God rather than disappointing Him by sinning. Did you know that even Jesus got angry?" Katy had heard so much about being angry and controlling her temper in the past but this was news to her. Her eyes widened as if to say, 'He did'?

"That's right, Jesus got angry . . . but He never sinned. You see, God knows that we will get angry too sometimes. The Bible never tells us not to get mad, it just says not to sin when we feel that way. The careless words that we may say and the actions that we do while angry are the times when we hurt ourselves and others the most. That kind of hurt can take a long time to heal." Mom was silent for a few minutes as she let Katy soak up what she had said.

After a long pause, Katy finally spoke. "Mommy, I'm

sorry for what I did. I know you and Daddy tell me to control my temper, but sometimes when I'm mad, I forget the 'control' part and just remember the 'mad' part."

Mom smiled at the innocent way Katy had of saying things. She knew Katy was genuinely sorry for what she had done. She also understood how hard it was to remember so many things as a child. Learning to control one's temper can be a very hard lesson, thought Mom, as she accidentally spilled her lemonade on her brand new magazine. "Drats!" cried Mom. Katy laughed as she and her mom hugged, then Katy went to apologize to her brother.

Let's Talk About the Story

Where were Katy and Kyle?

What was the problem in the story?

Did Kyle deserve the way Katy treated him and his belongings?

What does the Bible say about being angry? Is it a sin?

Prayer

Dear Father,

Thank you for being a patient and forgiving God. Thank you for not yelling at us and throwing our things away when we make mistakes. Help us to be kinder to others and not sin when we are mad. Thank you for understanding that we might get mad sometimes. Amen.

Family Activity

The next time you are angry, remember that your children are watching. They are like sponges and shadows, soaking in and copying everything we do. We are their mirror to the world. When you find yourself angry and reacting in a way that is not fitting for a Christian, take time to apologize to your children rather than defending what you did or said, whether they

are the brunt of your anger or not. Likewise, if something makes you mad but you have handled it well, explain the process you went through to help them understand that even moms and dads get angry, but you don't have to lose control of your emotions even when tempted to do so. Remember, whether it's someone cutting you off in traffic or the light taking too long to change, they see everything we do and will remember your actions much longer than they will your words.

References: Psalm 29:22; Psalm 29:11; Proverbs 15; Proverbs 29:11, Ephesians 4:26–27; 1 Peter 5:8

Week Four–"I Will Fear No Evil"

2 Timothy 1:7
For God did not give us a spirit of timidity, but a spirit of power, of love and of self-discipline. (NIV)

For God hath not given us the spirit of fear; but of power, and of love, and of a sound mind. (KJV)

It was 2:00 A.M. and nine-year-old Robyn was awake again. It was the third time this week that she had been awakened in her sleep by a frightening dream. Her dreams were so real to her that she was too afraid to walk by herself to her parents' room to get her mom and dad, so she just lay there as if frozen in ice. She would faintly cry out their names occasionally, but they could never hear her soft voice above the hum of the air conditioning. Tightly she clutched her favorite teddy bear named Coco and tried to think of happier times that weren't so scary. The night seemed to go on forever.

The next morning she was very tired. Of course she hadn't gotten much sleep during the night, but it was the lack of sleep she had been getting every night lately that was making her feel so tired and grouchy this morning. She didn't feel like going to school . . . again. She just wanted to stay in bed and hold Coco where it felt safe and warm. Her Dad was concerned about her as was her mom. But because Robyn was nine, she thought she was way too big to be getting scared at night, so she didn't tell her parents why she didn't feel like going to school. She decided it would be easier to get up and go, rather than risk her parents, sister, and brothers thinking she was a baby for always being scared. At school she had a good time playing with her friends, reading and writing creative stories, but during story time when her teacher, Mrs. Dewlin, read aloud to the class, she felt very sleepy and almost feel asleep. The teacher had noticed this for several days and finally called her Dad to let him know that it appeared Robyn wasn't getting enough sleep at night.

That night after her bath as her mom was tucking her in, she asked Robyn how she had been sleeping. Quietly, Robyn admitted that she wasn't sleeping very much lately because she kept having bad dreams. Her mom hugged her and held her close as tears ran down her cheeks. When Robyn's Dad came in the room, he sat on her bed too, wanting to find out what the dreams were about and comfort his daughter. As she snuggled Coco close to her chest, she told her mom and dad why she felt afraid and why she could never go get them at night, or even let them know the next day. Her fear of being embarrassed had also kept her from getting help. Robyn's mom and dad wanted to help their daughter. They didn't think she was being a baby or silly. They thought she had been very brave to have stayed in her room all alone, trying to handle her fears by herself, but they also wanted to give her some extra power in case she had another bad dream that made her feel afraid.

"Robyn, we hope you never have another scary dream or feel afraid even during the day," her dad began. "But everyone feels afraid from time to time. Being afraid isn't anymore silly than being happy or being sad is silly. Fear is just another feeling God has given us that lets us know something inside of us isn't comfortable. Our feelings are like mirrors. Just like a mirror reflects (or shows) an image in front of it, our feelings reflect (or show) what's going on inside our thoughts, sometimes even our dreams. God doesn't want His children to live in fear. He wants all of us to live in peace. He's given us many Bible verses that tell us so, and he's also given us His own Spirit to help comfort us when we're scared. When we're afraid, if we talk to God, that can help take our mind off of our scary thoughts and help us to think about something pleasant. God can replace our bad thoughts with good thoughts that aren't scary." Robyn was sitting in her dad's lap by now and started quietly crying as he spoke. He held her closer.

Her mom continued, "Robyn, talking to God won't automatically take away your fears forever, but it can help bring comfort for a time and maybe get you through a hard moment. I know it doesn't replace Daddy or me being with you and making you feel safe, but when we can't be with you, just remember that God is as close as a prayer." Robyn smiled at that then hopped into bed. Before turning out the light, her parents knelt down by her bedside and prayed with her, asking God to keep her safe and help her to rest peacefully during the night. They kissed her goodnight and then turned to leave.

Robyn had one more thing to add before falling asleep however, "Mom, Dad, thanks for not laughing at me. I know I can pray and God will hear me when I'm afraid, but just in case I still get scared, will you leave a light on and the door open a little, please?"

Let's Talk About the Story

Why was Robyn sleepy at school?
Why had she not told her parents about her bad dreams?
Did they make fun of her?
What did they say that helped her feel better?
Have you ever been afraid or had a bad dream?
Prayer
Dear Father,
Thank you so much for protecting us. Thank you for not

laughing when we are scared. Help us to feel peaceful when we sleep and when we do new things too. Help us never to laugh at others who are scared. Amen.

Family Activity

During a family gathering, sit on the floor with a mirror. Pass the mirror around and have each person make funny faces as they look at the reflection. Ask what they see and talk about what a reflection is and does, but keep it simple. Explain that our feelings are like the faces we make in a mirror; they are a reflection of us at the moment. Talk about a time when you felt afraid and how you handled it. Remember to be honest as you share your feelings with your children. They can learn a great deal from how we handle situations.

References: Psalm 27:1; Psalm 56:3; Psalm 91; Proverbs 3:24–26; Isaiah 40: 31; Matthew 6:34; 2 Corinthians 12:9; 1 Peter 5:7; 1 John 4: 4, 18

November—Hip, Hip, Hooray! It's Thanksgiving Day

During the month of November, we celebrate the Thanksgiving holiday. This tradition began when the Pilgrims came to America in 1620. That was a very long time ago. As they made their trip from Holland to America, many people died and even more became ill. Those who survived were excited to land at Plymouth Rock and have land under their feet rather than the rocky seas. The first winter in America was hard though. It was much colder than what they were used to back in England. They had to build their own houses, and they had little food to feed their families. Back then, the Pilgrims didn't have grocery stores, refrigerators, or stoves like we have today. All their food had to be grown or hunted and it wouldn't last long since they couldn't store it in a freezer. Many more people died during the first winter because of the harsh conditions.

The Pilgrims weren't the first people to live in America though. Others had lived here before them. Indians had lived in America long before the Pilgrims ever thought about leaving England for the New World. The Indians who had lived on the land for a very long time were excellent hunters and farmers. They were very nice to the Pilgrims and showed them how to hunt and grow their own food. The Pilgrims taught the Indians how to speak English and how to read and write. When the first fall came and much food had been grown and harvested, the Pilgrims had plenty of food for a change. They decided to have an enormous feast and invite their friends the Indians to dinner. The Pilgrims gave God thanks for all of His blessings during the past year. They thanked Him for health, for friends and family, for healthy food, and for shelter. That is why we celebrate

Thanksgiving today. We are taking time out of our busy schedules to say "thank you" to God. Without God meeting our needs, we wouldn't have the important things that we need to live well each day. God promises to meet our needs and He always does. God wants us to be glad for what He gives us. It makes Him happy to hear us say "thank you." We can also learn to praise God for who He is. We can be thankful for the way that He guides us too and keeps from making mistakes that could hurt us. Even if it's not Thanksgiving Day, we should always try to have an attitude that says "thank you."

This month as you learn about Thankfulness, see if you can pass the "thanksgiving test" and live each day feeling thankful for something you have.

Let's Talk About Thanksgiving

Who celebrated the first Thanksgiving?
What did the Pilgrims thank God for?
Name five things that you can thank God for.

Week One–Praise Him, Praise Him!

Psalm 118:24
This is the day the Lord has made:
let us rejoice and be glad in it. (NIV)

This is the day which the Lord hath made;
we will rejoice and be glad in it. (KJV)

"Praise Him, Praise Him, all ye little children. God is love, God is love. . ." The children choirs sang in their best singing voices ever. All the adults in the church heard their angelic sound ringing with the bells. It was a good reminder to everyone that the reason we praise God is because He IS love. But Victoria was confused. She thought about it during the rest of the service and thought about how she could ask her dad her important question when church was over.

"Daddy, how can we "raze" God? I thought He already was raised from the dead? Isn't that what Easter is about?" Obviously, Victoria didn't understand the words to the song that the children had sung in church. Her father explained the correct words and smiled at his five-year-old. "Daddy, then what does 'praise Him' mean?" How do we Praise God anyway? Daddy thought that was a very good question. He had to think about it himself before he answered.

Finally he answered, "Victoria, praising God means to think about God and all of His goodness. It means to tell Him you like who He is and want to worship only Him. God honors our praise and wants us to praise Him each and everyday. Only God is worthy of our praise, so He is disappointed if we give our heart of praise to another person rather than Him. That makes Him sad."

"Is praise like praying to God?"

"Yes," her dad answered, "it can be. We can praise God in our prayers, in singing and in our conversations that we have with our friends. Praise can go to God in lots of ways. It doesn't matter to God where we praise Him or when we praise Him. He doesn't even care how or what time we praise Him. What's important though is that we remember to bring our praise to Him."

"Okay, but, why do we praise Him, Daddy, just because He says to?"

"We should praise God because WE want to, not just because God wants it and has earned it. We can praise God because He loves us, or because He is love. We can also praise Him because He created us and made everything for us to enjoy. We can praise Him because of His kindness and gentle ways. Those are some very good reasons to praise Him. No one is like God. Nobody is as patient as He is. No one is as kind or forgiving as He is either. There's nobody in all the world that loves us like God does and provides for our needs. We can never run out of reasons to praise God. Sometimes adults get too busy and need to be reminded of that. That's why the song was so good to hear today at church. We all need to remember the many reasons we have to praise God."

"I think I like that song. Can we sing it together right now? Praise Him, Praise Him, all ye little children, God is love, God is love. . . ."

Let's Talk About the Story

Why did Victoria ask her dad the question about the song?
What was her question?
How often can you praise God?
Is God selfish to want us to praise him?

Prayer

Dear Father,

We want to praise you just for who you are. You are awesome God. You are great and holy. Thank you for being who you are. Thank you for being love and for loving us. Help us to remember to praise you more. Amen.

Family Activity

Have each person name something they like about each family member. Ask the person being complimented how it makes them feel to hear so many nice things. Then, ask them to name some things that they like about God. Tell them that it makes God feel good just like it makes us feel good to hear people talking nice about us. Remind them that there is a difference in complimenting others and praising them the way we praise God. Our true praise should be reserved for God and God alone.

References: Psalm 8:1; Psalm 9:1–2; Psalm 66; Psalm 92; Psalm 100: 5; Psalm 103:1–5; Psalm 107:1

Week Two–Answered Prayer

Psalm 107: 1
Give thanks to the Lord, for he is good;
his love endures forever. (NIV)

O give thanks unto the Lord, for he is good: f
or his mercy endureth for ever. (KJV)

The mail had just arrived. There was a letter for Mrs. Kinamon, Andrew's mom. She opened it and then looked up at her husband. In her hand she held a check she had been praying for. Mr. and Mrs. Kinamon smiled at each other and then thanked God for His blessings.

When they had finished, Andrew asked, "Mom, why did you do that?"

"Why did I do what, Andrew," she wanted to know?

"Why did you and Daddy say thank you to Jesus when it's not even suppertime or bedtime? Are you getting ready for bed?"

"Oh no, son," replied Mommy. "I just received some money in the mail that Daddy and I had been praying for. We wanted to tell God 'thank you' as soon I had received it to let Him know how grateful we are that He answered our prayers."

"But couldn't you have waited until we ate or went to bed. Don't you say your prayers at night, too?"

"Yes, we could have waited until either one of those times, but we were so happy that we didn't want to wait to tell Him thanks. When you receive a present for your birthday, you tell the person that gave it to you thank you as soon as you have opened it. You don't wait until dinner time or right before going to bed to call and say 'thanks' when they were with you at the time you opened it. Since God is with us all the time and sees everything we do, He knows when we receive a special gift from Him and He knows how happy it makes us. He wants to hear our prayer of thanks, just like others want to hear that we appreciate the present they give us on our birthday."

Daddy knelt down beside Andrew. "Andrew, we don't have to wait until dinner or bedtime to talk to God. We can talk to Him anytime we want to, no matter where we are. We can pray silently or aloud. It doesn't matter to God, He hears us no matter how we pray. When we give Him thanks for all the good things He has given us, it makes Him happy. We call those good things, 'blessings' or 'gifts.' God gives us all so many wonderful blessings that it would be selfish of us NOT to tell Him thank you. Besides, if we waited until the end of the day to thank Him for everything, we might forget all the gifts He had given us."

"What kinds of gifts does He give us, Daddy? I've never seen a present with a bow on it from God."

"Well, there are many different kinds of gifts we receive from our Heavenly Father," Mother said. "He gives us life and breath, food and water, shelter from the cold weather, and shoes for our feet. He gives us jobs and money to pay for things, crayons to color pretty pictures, toys to play with and baseball gloves to catch Daddy's fast balls."

"And He also gives us the beautiful mountains, the pretty sunset that we saw last night, the stars in the sky and all the trees that are in our backyard," Daddy added.

"Wow! There *are* a lot of things He gives us. I didn't know all those things were gifts from God. They don't even need a bow on them! They look good just like they are!" shouted an excited Andrew.

"Yes they sure do, son. There are so many wonderful blessings from God, even if we tried to count them all, we could never do it. We'd run out of time before we ran out of things to thank God for. Just remember Andrew, that every time you receive a special blessing from God, something that makes you feel good on the inside and happy on the outside, you can thank God for it, right where you are."

"I want to pray right now. Can I, Mom?" With that, all

three bowed their heads and held hands as Andrew prayed. "Dear God, thank you for the trees, and the flowers, and for crayons and forks and spoons, for baseball gloves and bats, and for my pillow and for Mommy and Daddy and my bike. Amen."

Let's Talk About the Story

Why did Mommy and Daddy bow their heads and pray when the mail arrived?

What did Andrew think about that?

When does God want us to pray?

Name five things you are thankful for today?

Prayer

Dear Father,

Thank you so very much for all the good gifts you have given us. Thank you for families and friends, for sunshine, swimming pools, and snow. Thank you for loving us so much that you give us nice things to enjoy. Help us to always be thankful of your gifts to us. Amen

Family Activity

Plan a time when you can take a walk outside as a family. Talk about all the things you see that God has given us to enjoy. Even if you live in the city, you can thank God for cars and buses that take you to work and for jobs that help to pay the bills. Take time after the walk to stop and pray outside, thanking Him for His blessings. When you come back in, have the kids write down (depending on their age and ability) 20 things they are thankful for. Then on another night, talk about these blessings.

References: Psalm 118: 24; 1 Corinthians 15:57; Philippians 1:3; James 1:17

Week Three–God's Great Guidance

Psalm 32:8
I will instruct you and teach you in the way you should go; I will counsel you and watch over you. (NIV)

I will instruct thee and teach thee in the way which thou shalt go: I will guide thee with mine eye. (KJV)

It was 11:00 at night. The stars were shining bright in the dark night sky and the moon's imperfect circle gave a glow to travelers on the road. The Clifton family was on their way to celebrate Thanksgiving with grandparents and cousins. It had been a long day. Mr. Clifton was getting tired, but he knew they should be arriving at their destination soon so he didn't want to stop. After a while, he realized he had made a wrong turn and didn't exactly know where he was. The vehicle he was driving was low on gas and most things were already closed for the night. Mrs. Clifton took out the map to see if she might be able to help get them back on the right road. Sure enough, within a few minutes, the family was headed in the right direction. The Clifton's arrived at Grandma and Grandpa's house safely without running out of gas. All the children had fallen asleep long before, but they were wide awake once the SUV came to a stop in front of the house they knew and loved so well. Squeals of delight and many hugs abounded as cousins, grandparents, and aunts and uncles who had been waiting up for their arrival greeted them outside.

The next morning as Barrett, Britton, and Brandon's parents began talking about their experience driving at night, they heard them say, "We were completely lost. We pulled over and asked God to guide us to the right road and help us find our way here. Within minutes we were going in the right direction again."

Eight-year-old Britton couldn't help but ask, "Mom, how

did God guide us here? Did He send a star like He did with the wise men when Baby Jesus was born?"

"No dear, not that way. God guides people in different ways, but last night He chose to use the help of a map with good sense from your father to get us on the right road. Last night when we got lost, God reminded me that we had a map in the car that I had put in right before we left our house. That was God taking care of us even before we were lost. Then, when we were lost and it was hard to see with no street lights available, God provided the light from the moon and stars to find the road we found on the map. The light in the sky was just enough to help us get back to where we needed to be," Mom replied.

Dad said, "Because we knew that God had directed us and showed us the right way, we stopped and gave thanks to Him for guiding us here safely. God guides us when we are lost like we were last night, but He also guides us when we feel confused on the inside and don't know the best decision to make. He will show us the right way to go and the best path for our lives if we ask and trust Him to lead us. God guides us by His spirit, by the Bible, by other Christians, and by prayer. Sometimes even by a star as He did in Bethlehem the night Jesus was born. When God guides us, we need to remember to tell Him thank you for His protection and leading us, just like we did last night."

"Mom," said Brandon, "I'm glad God sees everything we do because then He knows that we are lost and need His help."

"Yeah," agreed Barrett and Britton. Ten-year-old Barrett continued, "To me, God seems like the lantern that we use when we go camping. He helps us find our way if we keep Him beside us all the time. Is that right?"

"Kids," replied Mom, "I couldn't have said it better myself."

Let's Talk About the Story

Where were the Clifton's going?

What happened on the way there?
What did Mom and Dad do once they found their way?
How are some ways that God can guide us?

Prayer

Dear Father,

Thank you for always guiding us. Thank you for protecting us and keeping us from danger when we are lost. Help us to follow you like the wise men followed the star to see Baby Jesus. Amen.

Family Activity

Talk about times when you or the kids were lost and how that felt. Ask how they eventually found their way home or tell your story to them. Explain to them by using a flashlight, lantern, candles or the lights in the sky, how God can guide us by directing us down the right path when we are in need of direction. He will give us wisdom to follow the right path if we trust in him.

References: Proverbs 3:5–6; Psalm 23:2; Psalm 25:9; 2 Corinthians 2:14

Week Four–Attitude of Gratitude

Ephesians 5:19–20
Sing and make music in your heart to the Lord, always giving thanks to God the Father for everything*, in the name of our Lord Jesus Christ. (NIV)

Speaking to yourselves in psalms and hymns and spiritual songs, singing and making melody in your heart to the Lord; Giving thanks always for all things unto God* and the Father in the name of our Lord Jesus Christ. (KJV)

Have you ever been told that you need to be more grateful for something? Has your mother or father told you that you need to change your attitude? Being ungrateful means that someone doesn't appreciate what they have, no matter how nice a gift it may be. In other words, it means that someone doesn't seem happy or proud for what they have, what they have been given, what someone does for them or for how hard another person works to take care of the needs of others. People who are grateful say "thank you" often when others do something for them or give them something. No matter how small a gift it may be, those who show gratitude do so without thinking that a gift is "too small." They are happy just because they know someone was thinking of them.

In the book of Luke, the Bible tells a story about being grateful. In the story, Jesus meets ten men who are very sick. No one wants to be around them because of their disease, but when Jesus sees them and hears them asking to be healed, He does so without even thinking about it. He was happy to heal them. As they left Jesus to head back home, only one man turned around to thank Him for making him well. Jesus noticed and asked where the other nine were, but He knew the answer. They didn't care enough to take the time to thank Jesus; they only cared about what He could do for them. When He had done what they wanted, they didn't need Jesus anymore. Only one man said "thank you" when Jesus had healed all ten.

Have you ever been like one of those nine men and not thanked someone who did something extra nice for you or gave you something special? If so, you have been ungrateful. People need to be told "thank you," but so does God; each and every day. We need to have an attitude of gratitude towards God and for those He has put in our lives. A thankful spirit tells others that we love God with all our heart. It also tells others that we think they are important. We can show gratefulness to others by telling them thank you, by doing nice things for them, by obeying what they say even if we don't like it, and by praying for them. We can show God a grateful spirit by telling Him thank you, by praising Him, by serving others and by giving to the church. There are many ways we can say "thank you" to God. Let's not be like the nine men who were too busy and too selfish to tell God thank you. Let's be like the one who returned with joy to the feet of Jesus, praising Him for what He had done.

Let's Talk About the Story

What does it mean to have a grateful attitude?

What happened in the Bible story of the ten sick men?

What does God want us to do?

What has someone done nice for you today? Did you tell them thank you?

How can you show God you appreciate what He has done for you?

Prayer

Dear Father,

Thank you for never being too busy for us. Thank you for loving us and for always being with us. Help us to learn to be more grateful to others. Help us to be more grateful to you, too. Amen.

Family Activity

Sit down together and talk about something nice each person has done for another person in the family today or in the past week. Ask if they remembered to say thank you. Talk about some wonderful blessings God has provided for your family or each member in the past day/week and check to make sure that everyone recognized God at work and then thanked Him for it. Remember, kids are still learning. They won't recognize something being of God unless you as parents tell them and demonstrate a thankful spirit yourself. Let them hear you praising God and thanking Him often, not just at the dinner table. God is not limited to meals, and children need to learn that too. God wants our praise for Him to incorporate every moment of our day. Just by maintaining a grateful spirit goes a long way in witnessing to our children about our own views of God and our own attitude towards what He has done for us. Check yourself and see if you need to learn to be more grateful. Do you have a bad attitude that needs adjusting or are you modeling an attitude of gratitude?

References: Psalm 8:9; Psalm 9:1–2; Psalm 28:7b; Psalm 95:1–2, 6–7; Ephesians 5:18; Colossians 3:16

December—Giving From the Heart

What is your favorite time of year? Is it summer? Winter? Going back to school? Or, would it be Christmas? Most boys and girls love Christmas the most. The Christmas lights are beautiful. The music is fun to sing. The food is yummy and it's fun to play in the snow! But, the gifts are nice too, aren't they? Even adults like to receive gifts. Seeing the tree lined with gifts underneath is especially fun. It's kind of magical to dream about what could be awaiting your eyes as you open the gifts addressed to you on Christmas Eve or Christmas Morning. But, isn't it also exciting to go shopping for someone else too and to help wrap their gift and place it under the tree? Knowing you have a secret that they don't know about yet makes it even more fun. Receiving gifts is certainly fun, but giving gifts and seeing faces light up with surprise and happy thoughts makes giving even more fun. It gives a nice, warm feeling on the inside of our hearts that says, "Wow, this is really cool!"

It's sad though that as fun as giving is, most people act like Christmas is only about getting gifts and telling their mom and dad everything that they want. Christmas is about much more than opening up presents. Christmas is about giving. It's about giving gifts to others. It's about giving love and hope to others. It's about giving praise to God for sending His only son to earth as a baby so that we can live with Him someday in heaven. That's what Christmas is really about. All the other stuff is great fun, and it's okay to have fun at Christmastime, but we never should get so busy having fun that we forget to thank God for the Christ Child.

This whole month of December, all of the stories will be talking about giving to God. There are many ways that we can give to God and many different gifts we can give him. As you listen to the stories and memorize the Bible verses, remember to think of Jesus, the greatest gift of all.

Let's Think About Giving

What are some things you like the most about Christmas?

What is one of your favorite Christmas songs?

Find out what one of your parent's favorite songs is.

Christmas is about more than opening presents, it is about what?

Who gave us the greatest gift of all?

Week One–Sacrificial Giving

Malachi 3:10

Bring the whole tithe into the storehouse, that there may be food in my house.* "Test me in this," says the Lord Almighty, "and see if I will not throw open the floodgates of heaven and pour out so much blessing that you will not have room enough for it." (NIV)

Bring ye all the tithes into the storehouse, that there may be meat in mine house,* and prove me now herewith, saith the Lord of hosts, if I will not open you the windows of heaven, and pour you out a blessing, that there shall not be room enough to receive it. (KJV)

Samuel came home sad from church. He had not had any money to put into the offering in Sunday School like some of the boys and girls did. As he was sitting on the couch with his grandmother, she asked him why he looked so sad. He was afraid to tell her. Finally, after thinking about it for long time, he told her.

Samuel's grandmother, who took him to church with her every Sunday, had not thought about Samuel putting money in the offering plate as she did each week. She had done so most of her life and remembered the thrill as a child of placing a few coins into the church collection plate each week. "Samuel, I am so sorry I didn't think about that. I wish I would have remembered so that you wouldn't have had to remind me. I think we can take care of that for you. Your grandfather and I will make sure that you have money for the offering from now on."

Samuel smiled, and felt better. He had a few questions though. He wasn't sure he understood everything about giving. He knew his Sunday School teachers talked about it and said it was important. He knew that he wanted to give, but he wasn't sure he knew much else about the offering. "Grandma, can I ask you a question?" Of course, his grandmother was ready for any question he might have. "Why do you give an offering every week?"

"We give because God has given so much to us. It's our way of saying 'thank you' to God."

Samuel looked around the small, old farm house his grandparents lived in. It didn't have much furniture in it. It didn't have a computer or a new TV. In fact, even the car that they drove looked very old. She could see the confusion in his eyes.

"Oh, we don't have much compared to what others might have, but we have enough. We always have, and we have each other. That's all we need. God provides food for us and gives us a warm house, a car and friends that have been with us for years. That's more than enough to show gratitude towards God by giving our tithes and offerings to Him each week. Even if He hadn't given us these things, just the fact that He gave us his Son is enough for us to give Him a small amount of our money each week."

"But don't you need that money for groceries?" asked a curious Samuel.

"Absolutely not. God has always taken care of us. We've never missed a dime of that money. We both learned when we were very young that He wants us to give to Him. Giving a tithe is a command in the Bible, but God promises to give even more to us than we could ever give back to Him if we will trust Him. We decided when we got married that we would always give our tithes and offering. We've been doing it ever since and God's been blessing. But, the true blessing is in giving, Samuel. We give joyfully because we want to. That's what makes it so much fun."

Samuel smiled again and snuggled up to his grandmother. The heater wasn't working and it was a bit chilly in the old house, but Samuel decided that the warmth he felt in his heart for his grandparents made up for the lack of heat in the house. He couldn't wait to give to God. He knew, like his grandparents, that God had given him much more than he could ever give back to God.

Let's Talk About the Story

Why was Samuel sad?
Who did he go to church with each week?
Why did his grandparents give to God?
Did they ever miss the money they had given?

Prayer

Dear Father,
Thank you for giving so much to us. You give us everything we have and meet all of our needs every day. Even if we tried, we could never out-give you. Help us to give back to you joyfully and with a grateful heart for all that you have done for us. Amen.

Family Activity

Start a family commitment to giving. Have each person talk about what they want to give each week and sign a card. Don't forget to include yourselves in the commitment as well. Talk about what it means to tithe ten percent. Have each person name ways that God has met their needs—your family's needs in the past week. Play a game where you go around the room and each person must say one thing that God has provided for them. Do this without stopping for at least 5 minutes. See how many things you can come up with. Then ask, "Is it possible to ever out-give God?"

References: Proverbs 3:9

Week Two–Joyful Givers

2 Corinthians 9:7
Each man should give what he has decided in his heart to give, not reluctantly or under compulsion, for God loves a cheerful giver. (NIV)

Every man according as he purposeth in his heart, so let him give; not grudgingly, or of necessity; for God loveth a cheerful giver. (KJV)

Next Sunday was the last day for the missions offering to be collected at church. The money that was given would be sent to help missionaries in other countries tell boys and girls about God's love. Bethany had been excited to save her money for the offering. All of her friends had already given. Her brother and sister had also given their money. In fact, the whole family had decided to give to the missions offering in place of going skiing in the month of December. The money that they would have used to pay for skiing would be given to the church missions offering. That was the agreed upon plan and everyone had done their part. Now it was time for Bethany, but Bethany had changed her mind. When she saw her money filling her bank, she thought of a hundred other things she would rather do with that money. After all, she thought, it was her money. She should be able to use it however she wanted to, right? She didn't tell her family her plan because she knew they would be upset, Instead, she kept it a secret and hid the bank under her bed so they wouldn't see that she hadn't taken the money to church yet. However, as Mrs. Bratcher was looking for Bethany's lost library book, she happened to find the bank in its hiding place. She was surprised!

Bethany cried as her parents talked to her about the money, the lying, and the offering. She told them all the things she wanted to buy and how it didn't seem fair.

"Bethany, everyone had something they would like to have done differently with their money," her dad said, "but we agreed to give it to the church. So we did. However, you aren't being very cheerful about your part in giving to the missions offering. God doesn't want our money if we are going to give with a selfish attitude. He wants us to give joyfully. He wants us to WANT to give because we love Him, not because we feel forced to."

Mr. and Mrs. Bratcher left the room. They told their daughter that she could choose what to do with her money, but if she gave it, she should do so with a cheerful heart, not with an attitude that felt angry about giving it all away.

The next Sunday at church, they watched Bethany place all of her money in the collection plate at church. She had decided to give her money away in order to help others who didn't have as much as she had. Her parents noticed a smile on their daughter's face. She had made a hard decision, but it was clear that she felt good about what she had done. After church she told her mom and dad, "I'm glad I gave my money away. Those toys I wanted to buy would probably be broken or lost soon anyway. You were right. Giving does feel good. No wonder God loves a cheerful giver. It feels a lot better to give when you want to than when you are mad about it. I think I will try to give even more next year. Maybe I should start saving now."

Let's Talk About the Story

What was the problem in the story?

What did Bethany want to do with her money?

How does God want us to give our money?

Prayer

Dear Father,

Thank you for being patient with us as we learn how to give cheerfully. Thank you for giving so much to us. Help us to give with a joyful spirit no matter what it is that we give. Amen.

Family Activity

Try a plan like the Bratcher's did in the story. Come up with something that your family can sacrifice for the sake of a missions offering or a charity. Set a date when the money will be collected and turned in. Talk about how it feels to give collectively to a good cause. Afterwards, find out how each person felt when they gave the money.

References: Luke 6:38; Acts 20:35; 2 Corinthians 8:7, 12

Week Three–Sharing from the Heart

Matthew 6:19–21

Do not store up for yourselves treasures on earth, where moth and rust destroy,* and where thieves break in and steal. But store up for yourselves treasures in heaven . . . *for where your treasure is . . . there your heart will be also. (NIV)

Lay not up for yourselves treasures upon earth, where moth and rust doth corrupt,* and where thieves break through and steal; but lay up for yourselves treasures in heaven, where neither moth nor rust doth corrupt and where thieves do not break through nor steal: *for where your treasure is, there will your heart be also. (KJV)

The fire truck was pulling away. The late night fire was finally out and everyone was returning to their homes—everyone except the Thompsons. It was their house that had caught fire; now they had no home to return to. They were scared when the fire first broke out, then they were in shock. Now the family just felt tired. They were exhausted after a night of so much emotion. Friends from church had offered them beds at their house for the night, so they were preparing to leave. It was only three days before Christmas. All the presents had already been bought and wrapped awaiting the squeals of delight from Aubrey and Shelby, the two Thompson girls. But at the moment, pretty packages filled with surprises didn't seem so important anymore.

The next day, Mr. and Mrs. Thompson awoke early. Their friends, the Youngs, had coffee ready so they sat together sipping coffee and talking about the night before. Shortly, Aubrey and Shelby walked into the room that was so beautifully decorated with colorful Christmas lights and ornaments and sat with their parents on the sofa. "Mom, what are we going to do about Christmas? All of our presents were under the tree," said a sad Aubrey.

Mrs. Thompson hugged her daughter then said, "Honey, those gifts that were so important yesterday just don't mean anything to your daddy and me this morning. We're so happy that we got out safely and that we still have you."

"But we don't have any more money to buy you new presents," said five-year-old Shelby. It won't seem like Christmas without having a present to give you. Shelby began to cry. Her dad picked her up and put her on his lap.

"Shelby, until last night, presents were important to all of us, but now we don't care about presents. We don't have to have any gifts from you girls. Having all of us together this Christmas will be the best gift of all." Daddy held his daughter close and looked at his wife.

"It's fun to give presents to each other, but God has given us something better. He reminded us how important life is. It is so much better than the gifts under the tree. Those gifts will break, or burn, or get lost in a few weeks, but the gift of each other will last a lifetime. I'd much rather have this gift than any-thing else in the world." Mom looked happy, not sad, when she said that.

Aubrey and Shelby thought about their parents' words. Then eight-year-old Aubrey said, "I guess that makes sense. The fire was scary. I didn't like feeling that way, especially when I thought that Daddy was still in the house getting our cat, Oreo. If I have to choose just one thing, I would choose having my family with me too."

"Girls, I know this is going to be a hard time for all of us, but we have so much to be thankful for. In fact, even though we don't have gifts to share with one another, we have our time and our talents we can give to each other this Christmas."

"That's right," said Mom. Why don't we plan to give each other the gift of ourselves this year? Maybe you girls could come up with a play or sing some songs for us and we could record it. And since we all know what it's like to be without a place to live, we could give our time to the homeless shelter. We may not have a house right now, but we do have friends who will let us stay with them. Some people don't have friends that they can live with so they end up living under bridges and on the street. God has been good to us; I think it would be good if we returned His blessings by sharing from what we do have."

All of the Thompsons and the Youngs thought that was a great idea. Everyone was happy and laughing. Soon they were making plans for one of the best Christmases any of them had ever had. That year they all learned a little more about giving from the heart and what the real value of a gift is.

Let's Talk About the Story

What happened to Aubrey and Shelby's house?
Where did they stay the first night?
What were the girls concerned about?
What is more important than gifts under the tree?

Can you think of some ways you can give to others this holiday that doesn't involve spending any money?

Prayer

Dear Father,

Thank you for protecting us from dangers all around. Thank you for looking out for us. You have taught us the real value of a gift and what is important in life. Help us to remember that having each other, and having you is better than any gift under the tree. Help us to be grateful for everything you have given us. Amen.

Family Activity

Plan a birthday party for Baby Jesus sometime during the season. Decorate for a birthday party and invite friends to come. However, instead of exchanging Christmas gifts with each other, have everyone bring a new or favorite used toy, wrapped, to give to a homeless shelter. Then, before the party is over, deliver the gifts to the boys and girls who need them. See the smiles that come across the faces of those receiving the gifts, but also on the faces of those giving them. It truly is much better to give than to receive.

References: Matthew 6:3–4; Luke 6:38; Acts 20:35; Romans 12:6–8; Philippians 4:19; 1 Peter 4:10

Week Four–The Greatest Gift

Luke 2: 10–11

But the angel said to them "Do not be afraid. I bring you good news of great joy that will be for all the people. Today in the town of David a Savior has been born to you: he is Christ the Lord. (NIV)

And the angel said unto them, Fear not: for, behold, I bring you good tidings of great joy, which shall be to all people. For unto you is born this day in the city of David a Saviour, which is Christ the Lord. (KJV)

"It's the most wonderful time of the year. . . ." the song continued on the radio. Ten-year-old Holly sang along. She loved the song as much as she enjoyed this time of year. It was her favorite season because of the fun songs, the pretty lights, the Christmas trees, and the television specials. But she also liked hearing the story of Baby Jesus over and over again. She never got tired of hearing about the angels telling the shepherds of the miracle that came to earth and of them finding Jesus in the manger. She had often thought how neat it would be if she could have been there to see the Baby Jesus and Mary and Joseph in the stable. Holly was happy it was Christmas. Then one night when her dad was reading a Christmas story to her and her sister Natalie, he said something she had never thought of before. He said that Jesus was the greatest gift ever given. Jesus was a gift? How could that be? He didn't come wrapped in a bow and placed under a tree did He? Then how could He be a gift?

Mr. Dickerson continued on with his thought as his two young daughters listened carefully. "We all love to receive gifts don't we? We like the surprise as much as the present itself it seems. But giving is as much a part of Christmas as receiving is. God knew that. That's why He gave us His son, Jesus. Jesus didn't come wrapped in pretty paper and lying under a twinkling tree. Instead, He came wrapped in swaddling clothes, lying in a manger, underneath a twinkling sky. He didn't come to be tossed away and forgotten in a few weeks like we do our presents; He came to give us life that lasts forever. I can't think of a better Christmas present than one that lasts forever, can you?"

Six-year-old Natalie's eyes were wide with wonder. She had never thought of that either. Jesus was a gift. He was God's gift to us. Her father continued, "He didn't come wrapped as we would wrap presents or found in a place we expect to find gifts, but He came as a surprise to the world one dark, cold night. And just like our gifts bring joy to others, the gift of Jesus brings joy too, but His joy lasts a lifetime.

"Wow!" said Holly. "Dad, if God did all that for us, what do we have to do for Him? Don't we need to get Him a present too?"

"Holly, God's gift of Jesus is a free gift to anyone who will receive it. God receives the joy when we receive the gift of His Son, Jesus. We can't do anything to repay God. Anything we would try to do would never match such a great gift. All God wants of us is to serve and love Him."

"That's it? But that sounds too easy. If I were God and I gave my son away, I would want people to pay something back, especially if He died for them." Holly couldn't believe what her father was telling her.

"Holly, there's nothing we can do. You can't earn salvation or hope that if you are good enough God will love you more than someone else and let you into heaven. God knew when He gave His Son that it was a priceless gift. That's why it is free. God only asks those that accept His son as the only way of salvation to love Him with all their hearts."

"Daddy, I want to do that. I want to follow Jesus and love Him. I believe that God sent Jesus as His son and died on the cross. What else do I need to do?"

"I'm glad you asked, sweetie. Your mom and I have been praying for you for a long time. All you have to do to accept

Jesus into your heart is to pray. That's it. If you'd like, you can follow after me. Just say what I say and ask Jesus to forgive you and to come into your heart."

Mom, Dad, and Holly knelt beside the Christmas tree while Natalie sat quietly near by. Jingles, their dog lay beside Holly as she began to repeat after her father in prayer.

"Dear God, I know that I am a sinner. I know that you sent your only son as a baby to save me from my sins. I know I have done many things that are wrong. Please forgive me for my sins. Come into my heart and save me. I want to follow you. I love you God. Thank you for giving us the greatest Christmas gift ever, your Son Jesus. Amen."

With tears in their eyes, Mr. and Mrs. Dickerson and Holly looked up. They hugged each other for a very long time. They knew this Christmas was going to be the best Christmas ever. For, like the shepherds and the wise men long ago, they had seen the star and followed it to find Baby Jesus, a gift like none other.

Let's Talk About the Story

What did Holly like about the season?

What did her father tell her about Jesus?

Holly wanted to do something after hearing her Dad tell the story. What did she want to do?

What is the greatest gift ever given?

Prayer

Dear Father,

Thank you for the gift of your son. Jesus is the best gift ever! Help us to tell others about your gift with boldness, with joy, and with hope. We love you Jesus. We want to follow you. Amen.

Family Activity

Talk about the best presents each person has ever received. Talk about how it made you feel and why? Then ask where that present is now and what became of it. Relate that to Jesus as the gift that never goes away.

References: Isaiah 9: 6; Matthew 1:21; I John 4:9–10

Memory Verse Checklist

	Jan	Feb	Mar	Apr	May	June	July	Aug	Sept	Oct	Nov	Dec
Week One	Gen. 1:1	Gal. 5:22-23	Rom. 5:8	Matt. 5:16	Is. 46:9	Eph. 6:1	Matt. 7:7	Jam. 4:4	Col. 3:23	Prov. 15:13	Ps. 107:1	Mal. 3:10
Week Two	Gen. 1:27	I Cor. 13:13	Eph. 2:8-9	Jam. 1:22	Heb. 1:3a John 14:6	Rom. 13:1	Ps. 119:105 Ps. 119:11	2 Tim. 2:23-24	Gal. 6:4-5	Ps. 34:18	Ps. 118:24	2 Cor. 9:7
Week Three	Ps. 139:14	Eph. 4:32	John 3:16	Matt. 28:19-20	John 14:26	Lev. 19:32	Ps.122:1	Matt. 7:12	Ps. 34:13-14	Ps. 4:4	Ps. 32:8	Matt.6: 19-21
Week Four	Rom. 10:12	I Pt. 5:8	Rev. 3:20	Matt. 6:14-15	I Pt. 1:15-16	I Pt. 2:17	Heb 11:6	2 Chron. 19:11 James 4:7	1 Cor. 15:58	2 Tim. 1:7	Eph.5: 19-20	Luke 2: 10-11

Contact author Robin Newman
or order more copies of this book at

TATE PUBLISHING, LLC

127 East Trade Center Terrace
Mustang, Oklahoma 73064

(888) 361 - 9473

Tate Publishing, LLC

www.tatepublishing.com